Stuff I've Been Feeling Lately

a collection of poems by

Alicia Cook

Andrews McMeel
PUBLISHING®

Dedication

This book is dedicated to anyone who
loves someone struggling
with addiction.

And, as always, to
Mom, Dad, and Michael

side A
the poems

Track One

This is dedicated to the man who saved me.

He didn't save me from a car wreck;
my existence managed to swerve off the road,
creating a mangled mess even the
Jaws of Life couldn't tear through.

He didn't save me from fiery flames.
Quite the contrary, and perhaps
even a bit more frightening, the fire inside
of me had long burned out.

He didn't save me from drowning,
at least not in the literal sense.
I can swim just fine and still the rip currents
of life took me under, and I began
to flounder in my own tears.

Simply, this is dedicated to the man who saved
me from the biggest catastrophe of all: *myself*.

Currently Listening To:
Ellie Goulding, "How Long Will I Love You?"

Track Two

You always want one more day.
You always want one more picture
as the old ones begin to fade.
You always want that one final hug
to have lasted just a tad longer.
You always want the fondness
of the *remember-whens*
to outnumber the *might-have-beens*.
You want more years, more months,
more weeks, more days,
more minutes, and more seconds.
You want the *happily ever after*
you always thought you deserved,
but the only thing actually promised
in this life is uncertainty.

Currently Listening To:
Rod Stewart, "Forever Young"

Track Three

I c o m b through my memories

with more
care than I do my hair.

I'm told the key is to preserve the root.

Still, I have difficulty remembering things.

I recall second natures

in

p
a
r
t
i
a
l
s,

never wholes.

I flip through photo albums
and see my likeness in someone
I can't manage to recognize anymore,
even when I squint.

She shares my fingerprints.
They tell me it's me.

It's as if I am wearing
hand-me-down memories
from a life that doesn't fit quite right.

They were a gift,
so squeeze into them.

I experience that familiar itch of frustration
as I struggle to name the girl in the photo.

Imagine the anguish felt
by having your very own existence
on the tip of your tongue.

Currently Listening To:
Sara Bareilles, "She Used to Be Mine"

Track Four

Yeah, she's beautiful.
Anyone with decent eyesight can tell you that.

That's not why I love her.

I love her when she is putting on her makeup,
sitting on the bathroom counter.

I love her when she makes me order
the Chinese or pizza
but constantly whispers the order
into my ear because she is convinced
I'll mess it up.

I love her when we are walking
and she trips over nothing on the sidewalk
and keeps talking, not missing a beat,
like it just didn't happen.

I love her when we are packing the car
for a trip and she hands me seven bags.

I love her when she is curled up
on our couch wearing my shirt.

I love her after her first sip of coffee
or her last sip of wine.

I love her when she first gets out of the shower
in the summer and I see her vivid tan lines.

I love her when she steals the covers all night
and then, come morning,
blames me for turning on the fan.

I love her when we drive during the holidays,
her feet up on the dashboard,
sipping hot chocolate and
looking at Christmas lights.

Currently Listening To:
Lee Brice, "A Woman Like You"

Track Five

She jumped from one happiness
to the next. *(You're the only one.)*

They made her smile
(You're beautiful)
until they made her cry
(But I'm not looking to settle down.)

They broke her heart *(This isn't
working anymore,)* and her spirit
(But let's still be friends.)

Over and over again,
she trusted the f r a g m e n t s
of her soul with others
(I'd never hurt you like he did.)

She thought they could fix her.
Once they inevitably abandoned her
(It's not you, it's me) she would end up
leaving with more of them than of herself.

And this is how a person's own reflection
can become unrecognizable.

Currently Listening To:
O.A.R., "Shattered"

Track Six

The strongest people I know
have been overtaken by their weaknesses.
They know what it's like to lose control.
The strongest people I know
have cried in the shower and in their car.
They know loss and guilt all too well.
The strongest people I know aren't bulletproof.
They have felt the searing pain of life's shots.
The strongest people I know
make the decision every day to wake up
and place their two feet on the ground
even though they know the monsters beneath
their bed will grab at their ankles.

The strongest people I know
are not *strong* by definition, at all.

They are mistake-makers.
They are mess-creators.
They are survivors.

Currently Listening To:
50 Cent, "In Da Club"

Track Seven

To Whom It May Concern:

Drive away. You don't live here anymore.

You are not home free if you are still calling this place Home. Check your mirrors. *Images are closer than they appear and not as pretty as they seem.* Those rose-colored sunglasses of yours are playing tricks on your eyes. This nostalgic route is messing with your heart. That familiar song on the radio has penetrated your mind.

Honestly, I hope you don't spend one minute missing me. Missing this. You will heal as long as you don't turn around. *Ever.* Sometimes even a glance into the past can kill you.

Sincerely,
The Girl You Used to Be

Currently Listening To:
The Weepies, "Can't Go Back Now"

Track Eight

She lost herself.

I'm talking *down-the-rabbit-hole-free-fall* like the little blonde girl in that book she read once. She was so far gone, even her own shadow kicked her when she was down. Friends and family would tell her she would be her *old self* in no time flat.

You'll find yourself again, they would say. They would promise her this in hopes she would find comfort in the possibility. They made it seem like a blessing. To her, the idea of becoming herself again felt more like a curse. Why would she purposely go hunting for that girl just to feel all the pain she had once felt?

Why? If that meant having the memories, mistakes, and regrets find her again, too? No, she didn't want to become her *old self* again.

If she survived her latest misadventure, she vowed to become someone entirely new.

Currently Listening To:
Rachel Platten, "Fight Song"

Track Nine

The first time my heart broke, I thought back to
the day in my childhood when a piece of glass went
through my finger after an ill-fated cartwheel.

I was eleven years old.

My mother and I were in our bathroom cleaning
up the wound. She dribbled peroxide onto the cut.
It fizzed and burned; I winced at the pain.

It needs to burn so you know it's healing,
she explained.

That small exchange during my adolescence helped
me learn to appreciate the pain pulsating from my
broken heart. In spite of the severity of my wound,
I knew the healing process had already begun.

Currently Listening To:
Big Sean, "Dark Sky (Skyscrapers)"

Track Ten

I had become accustomed to using moving boxes as makeshift coffee tables. I was never in one place for too long and always in my car longer than any bed; but there was an anomaly in that last drive.

It was one of those special car rides where every song on the radio was one of my favorites. The road was open and smooth, freshly paved.

And the thing is, I wasn't driving anywhere new. For once in my life, *home* had become a singular destination for me.

I regained my soul through you.
I regained my soul through our consistency.

Currently Listening To:
Sonny & Cher, "I Got You Babe"

Track Eleven

You can taste sorrow in salt tears and in the
bitterness of spoiled words left in your mouth
for far too long.

You can hear sorrow in a familiar song. You can
hide sorrow behind closed doors and inside
screams muffled by pillowcases.

You can stick to sorrow as if it were gum
in your hair; too mangled to brush out,
too jarring to chop off.

You can see sorrow in
bloodshot eyes and shaky hands.

You can get lost in sorrow when it knocks your life
off course with no detour signs to redirect you.

Most importantly,
you can be found in sorrow by
becoming a different version of yourself,
here, *on the other side* of tragedy.

Currently Listening To:
Bright Eyes, "Hit the Switch"

Track Twelve

My *new beginnings* have often spawned from
forced endings. With one of life's chapters being
ripped from my hands before I even had time to
dog-ear my favorite parts. For a very long time I
confused the notion of *a fresh start* with walking
toward distress instead of away from it.

Now, I relish the thought of
getting to know the unknown.
Getting to familiarize
myself with the unfamiliar.
Getting to start over smack dab
in the middle of my life
whenever I damn well please.

Currently Listening To:
Craig Mack feat. Notorious B.I.G., LL Cool J,
"Flava in Ya Ear (Remix)"

Track Thirteen

There has always been a d i s c o n n e c t
between me and the world around me;
I never felt settled, grounded.

Suddenly, it became so clear.
Perhaps I lost myself so often because
I found my sandy feet in a shore town.

All my life, my footprints were
repeatedly washed away by the tide,
as if I never existed there in the first place.

Currently Listening To:
Miranda Lambert, "Airstream Song"

Track Fourteen

Just because I don't trust you
     doesn't mean I have trust issues.
Just because I won't commit to you
     doesn't mean I have commitment issues.
Just because I watch what I eat
     doesn't mean I have body image issues.
Just because people have left my life
     doesn't mean I have abandonment issues.
Just because I yearn to grow and evolve
     doesn't mean I have identity issues.

I know exactly who the hell I am.

Currently Listening To:
Chris Brown feat. André 3000, Drake,
Fabolous, Kanye West, T.I., "Deuces"

Track Fifteen

A picture never fully captures
the reasons behind why I want
to freeze the moment
in the first place.

It doesn't capture the distant
smell of a fireplace burning as
it's quickly overtaken by the
unmistakable aroma of low tide.
It doesn't capture the cleansing
scent of salt air entering my nostrils.
It doesn't capture the monstrous
howl of the wind whipping through
my hair or the pleasurable
sting of the sand in my eyes.

It doesn't capture the transformation
in the texture of the sand beneath
my feet as I approach the breakers.
It doesn't capture the unexpected warmth
of November's ocean as it reaches my ankles.

The lens of a camera cannot capture any of that;
my heart does.

Currently Listening To:
Lady Antebellum, "Goodbye Town"

Track Sixteen

The *new normal* is rarely an easy adjustment and
never truly feels, well, *normal*.

Let's be honest.

Plan B is never preferred.
Detours and alternate routes
are never quite as scenic.

The darkness of being gifted a second chance
is that it means something went
wrong in the first place.

And yet,

I would rather have a few speed bumps slow me
down, causing me to spill coffee on my dress, than
ever hand someone else the keys to my life.

Currently Listening To:
Goo Goo Dolls, "Rebel Beat"

Track Seventeen

Sometimes you don't realize
you are h o l d i n g yourself
together until

you
aren't
anymore.

Suddenly, you're not the same
person you thought you were
j u s t   m o m e n t s before.

No.

You are not okay.
You are not fine.
But you will be.

When I say, *you will be okay,*
I do not mean you will wake up
one day and be the same person
you were before the pain.

Pain changes a person.

But, you will discover a
new version of yourself.

One who has experienced the great sadness
that only follows a great loss.

One who knows the
value of a good cry.

One who knows that even after
the coldest of winters,
spring will still arrive.

Currently Listening To:
Eminem, "'Till I Collapse"

Track Eighteen

We cleanse our palates as midnight resets our lives. Clean slates always taste better when fizzy. The unknown is easier digested when fizzy.

Currently Listening To:
Frank Sinatra, "The Best Is Yet to Come"

Track Nineteen

There are

lay
    ers

to loving me.

In the beginning, I am quite easy to love.
My surface is smooth, my smiles tender.

But as time undresses,
my insides are revealed to be rough and ragged.
It will become awfully difficult to love me.
At times, borderline impossible.

Many have left; for people would rather
see a car accident unfold from afar,
than be the shotgun rider.

Until you.

Only you can see all you see, know all you know
about me, and still look at me like *this*.

Currently Listening To:
Bright Eyes, "First Day of My Life"

Track Twenty

My lifelong person.
The man who will help
zip my dress every morning.

How do you do it?

You fix everything
time and time again
just by surviving
t h r o u g h the
moment with me.

Currently Listening To:
Pearl Jam, "Just Breathe"

Track Twenty One

If you are lucky enough to have a childhood friend, try your hardest to grow old with them. These friends are a unique, irreplaceable breed.

These friends lived through curfews and Polaroid pictures with you. These friends know your parents and siblings because they had to call your house first to speak with you. Your memories are not frozen in time on social media, but live on nonetheless.

Most importantly, they remember the person you were before the world got ahold of you, so they have this crazy ability to love you no matter what.

They are the living, breathing reflection of where you have been. And so, just when you think you've lost yourself for good, they are there to bring you face-to-face with your true self, simply by sharing a cup of coffee with them.

As your world grows and becomes larger and more complicated than your backyard, even if you establish a life elsewhere, I hope your childhood friends remain lifelong allies, because mine have saved my life on more than one occasion.

Currently Listening To:
The Beatles, "With a Little Help from My Friends"

Track Twenty Two

2015

I didn't just survive this year;
I lived it.

I laughed, I cried,
I scribbled things in journals.
My heart broke, but kept ticking.
My passport earned a few new stamps.

I had fancy Saturdays
and lazy Sundays.

I dipped my toes in tropical seas.
I hiked mountains
and cheated on my diet.

I made my twenty-ninth
consecutive birthday wish.

Because of this, and so much more,
I will never settle on simply
surviving ever again.

I choose to live.

Currently Listening To:
OneRepublic, "I Lived"

Track Twenty Three

I want you to know,
I love you the other 364 days, too.

All the commercially popular grand gestures in the
world could never compete with the millions of
everyday little things you have done, and continue
to do, for me. You continue to love me when I am,
by definition, unlovable. You continue to love me
when I don't particularly love myself. You allow
me to remain my quirky self in a world that prefers
conformity. I can only hope I bring to you the same
feeling of completeness and unconditional
acceptance that you have given to me.

Love isn't about tangible things.
Love has always been about two people.

And since we are only allotted one life per person,
I feel undeniably privileged and fortunate to get to
spend my one lifetime with you.

Currently Listening To:
Christina Perri, "Miles"

Track Twenty Four

For the first time
in months,
I didn't wear a jacket
on Sunday.

I woke up and felt *different*.

Even before I cracked open my windows, allowing
what definitely resembled a spring breeze to creep
through and ruffle the loose papers on my dresser.
Even before I heard birds chirping and a seagull
cawing overhead. Even before the aroma of freshly
ground coffee entered my nostrils, smelling more
like a pleasure than a necessity. It was as if my soul
had thawed. I felt completely reinvigorated.
Instead of wearing one of my seventeen pairs of black
yoga pants I had been wearing since October, I opted
for an olive green maxi dress and a light cardigan.
Others felt the change, too. I noticed some girls in
flip-flops hopscotching through puddles
of melting snow.

Call it ridiculous, but there was an upswing in my
mood, just at the mere promise of spring.

Perhaps my decision to nix the jacket was a symbol
for change, not just in the weather, but within
myself.

I caught a glimpse of the girl I had been missing greatly the last couple of months. It was nice to see her again.

So Sunday, I sang along with the radio really loudly and unapologetically, I drank three mimosas before one o'clock, and I didn't wear a jacket.

Currently Listening To:
Kendrick Lamar, "Bitch, Don't Kill My Vibe"

Track Twenty Five

I am never going to be the girl with the perfectly straightened hair or creased clothing. Even at my most put together, I'll look a bit d i s h e v e l e d.

My socks will never match, but no one will notice that except for my lover and airport security. At the most inopportune times, I'll have a run in my stocking or a runny nose.

I'll combine foods even a pregnant woman wouldn't crave. On way more than one occasion, my friends have said out loud, *I would not want to spend one minute in your head.*

I was always aware of what I encompassed. I have never tried to conform because I did not feel the pressure to do so *(thanks, Mom!)*. Yes, this self-assurance led to my grade school years being a living hell, but even then I recognized that time of my life as *temporary*.

I do not fear, nor am I ashamed of, myself.

As long as I am happy, it is my God-given right to be odd. To be my true self.

Currently Listening To:
Taylor Swift, "Mean"

Track Twenty Six

The way you peer
into my depths
with such ease,
my soul must
have a glass bottom.

You embrace
my complexity
and bravely swim
against my current.

You do not fear the pull of
my murky undertow.

You vow *forever* to me
as if it were as simple as
slipping a ring upon my finger
because, maybe this time, *it is.*

Currently Listening To:
Ed Sheeran, "Tenerife Sea"

Track Twenty Seven

Sometimes it hurts to breathe.

My corrupt decisions
weigh on my chest,
methodically pushing down
to crack each rib,
in hopes of infiltrating
my heart and finally exterminating
the last shred of the human being
I once was.

If that happens,
if my sanctuary is breached,
I will not stand a chance.

I will lose the one last single atom
that makes me, *me.*

I can't lose me.
I'm all I've got.

Currently Listening To:
Tupac, "Keep Ya Head Up"

Track Twenty Eight

Growing up, my mother cautioned I would
not possess the power to plan out my life.

I couldn't say,
I'll be married by X,
have a kid by Y,
have a book out by Z.

I was told as much as I crave to treat my life as one
big to-do list, I would instead find myself asking,
Where from here? at least a few times in my life.

Now, I catch myself asking this a few times a day.

Where from here?

Three pint-sized words shouldn't be able to pose
such a fatal and final question, but alas, they do. If
you go right, you can't go left. Even if you
backpedal to take the other route just a second
later, your fate will already be altered. It's this or
that, never both. It is a hard pill for me to
swallow, but I do believe it is in the navigation
that you find your way, and inevitably
find yourself.

Currently Listening To:
Miranda Lambert, "Mama, I'm Alright"

Track Twenty Nine

I carry you with me all of the time,
but I feel your absence most on the
days when I'm the happiest.

Not when I *need* you here the most,
but when I *want* you here the most.

I believe grief is like a shadow.

It's always there, it follows
you everywhere you go,
but you only see it when
the sun is shining on a beautiful day.

Currently Listening To:
The Band Perry, "If I Die Young"

Track Thirty

A change in the season
always ignited a change
in your heart.

I became angry with the Universe
and its natural transitions.

I came to fear
our altered rhythm;
the subtle shifts
in both your affection
and in the air.

Seasons
have
patterns.

You'd be back.

And like winter's
losing fight
against spring,

I'd thaw.

Currently Listening To:
Griffin House, "Tell Me a Lie"

Track Thirty One

EWR to BNA

The ride to the airport is always too short.

Even if I'm packed for days, I'm never ready to go.
A nervous feeling inhabits my stomach right before
my feet hit the hectic curb.

I check my bag and then head up to security. The
line is long as the employee asks, *Are you alone?*

(In life or just right now?)

He points me in the direction away from
the lovers and families traveling together.

The person in front of me doesn't have to
remove their shoes but I do (*of course*)
so now I'm barefoot in Newark Airport.

I make it to the gate
and immediately insert my headphones.

That doesn't stop the Chatty Cathy beside me
from asking, *So, where are you coming from?*

(Don't you mean, "What are you running from?")

Pretending she startled me, I remove my
headphones. She repeats the question.

(How specific do you want me to get? I'm coming from therapy. I'm coming from a weekend of binge drinking. I'm coming from a sleepless night due to a migraine I'm still feeling.)

I answer, *New Jersey.*

I've always preferred the more hopeful,
Where are you heading?

My answer?

Everywhere.

Currently Listening To:
Brand New, "Okay, I Believe You, but My Tommy Gun Don't"

Track Thirty Two

There have been nights
I've shared a twin bed with him
and still couldn't get close enough.

Then there have been nights
spent in a king bed where I've felt
as though his annoying ass was still
in my personal space.

We e b b and f l o w.
But there's no one else I'd rather
crash into every night when
the tide hits its inevitable peak.

Currently Listening To:
Des'ree, "I'm Kissing You"

Track Thirty Three

I feel at peace the nights
I find myself naked
beneath our sheets.

I stare at the ceiling,
and I create my own constellations
from its paint cracks.

I feel more connected to the Universe
during the moments we spend together
under our artificial plaster sky

than I ever could on evenings spent
outside, with the starry night sky,

counting actual
constellations

without you.

Currently Listening To:
Andrew McMahon in the Wilderness, "Cecilia and the Satellite"

Track Thirty Four

Not laughing for fear of crying.
Not loving for fear of heartbreak.
Not choosing for fear of wrong decisions.
Not dreaming for fear of nightmares.
Not trusting for fear of betrayal.
Not jumping for fear of broken bones.
Not exploring for fear of getting lost.

Not attempting for fear of failing
is like not living for fear of dying.

It is impossible to escape this world unscathed.

So, embrace this m e s s y,
un   certain   existence

and live.

Currently Listening To:
Kacey Musgraves, "Somebody to Love"

rack Thirty Five

I'm not the one who got away.

Late nights and loneliness
have built me up in your head.

Letting go of even the wrong heart
can play tricks on one's mind,
confusing two souls that
once mated for soul mates.

So, please, the next time
the smell of Chanel fills up a room
and you find yourself
reminded of me, remember:

I never even wore perfume.

Currently Listening To:
Nancy Sinatra, "Bang Bang (My Baby Shot Me Down)"

Track Thirty Six

I find comfort
in the colors of a sunset.

I find a special magic
in the fact
it never photographs
as beautifully as my eyes
can witness it firsthand.

I find a certain peace
in the conclusion of
another day lived.

And I find hope
in the precarious promise
of tomorrow.

Currently Listening To:
Lee Ann Womack, "I Hope You Dance"

Track Thirty Seven

Four children sit together in a room,
forming a square.

In the center is a deck of cards. Brand new.
Together, using all fifty-two, they construct a
house of cards.

They revel at their masterpiece for all of two
minutes, as one of their mothers enters the room.
Believing it to be muggy, she opens the window.

A gust of wind enters and blows
the cards in different directions.

Annoyed a tornado destroyed their work in mere
seconds, one child storms out of the room, leaving
the door open. The three remaining children
decide to start over.

Card by card the house is reassembled.
Immediately following, the family's puppy
charges into the room through the opened door
and plows into the house of cards like a
wrecking ball through cement.

Another one of the children runs out in tears.

The remaining two children once again collect the
fifty-two cards and begin to form the foundation.

And just as the final card is placed on top,
the mother reappears and swings the
playroom door closed.

Though brief, the sudden, manufactured airstream
causes the house to collapse for the third time just
as the door slams shut.

This setback causes another child
to march out of the room.

A single child begins gathering the cards.

Her mother comes in and asks why she is playing
alone when all her friends are outside.

Without even a hesitation, the child responds,
If I still have the pieces, why wouldn't I keep
rebuilding?

Currently Listening To:
Eminem, "Solider"

Track Thirty Eight

No matter how old I become, a slight sadness always washes over me moments before I drive away from the home where I grew up.

Feelings of melancholy enter the pit of my stomach as though I am saying goodbye to a dear friend. I stand at the curb soaking in the last moments of hearing my mother's wind chimes sway in the autumnal air.

It is likely I will live in a few different houses throughout my life, but I believe there will always only be one *home* for me.

A home where memories have seeped deep into the paint and pillows; where unconditional love travels around the house as if it were another member of the family.

A sanctuary where pictures, unchanged for years, hang on the wall as reminders of who I used to be and how far I have come.

There is something different about the breeze that passes through the windows of my parents' home; it somehow holds the power to wrap around me and rock me until I drift off to sleep.

That cozy security felt by sharing a bedroom wall
with my sister. There's something reassuring
about seeing my mother's purse slung over a
kitchen chair or my father's shoes
by the front door.

In a world where so many unfamiliar variables can
arise out of nowhere, it is a comfort to have a very
familiar constant.

Home: where love and support concurrently
grounded me and encouraged me to fly.

Currently Listening To:
Carrie Underwood, "Don't Forget to Remember Me"

Track Thirty Nine

I was running errands the day I received the worst news of my life. I got the phone call in Target's parking lot, hung up, got out of my car, puked on the side of my tire, and still walked into the store to buy the birthday card I needed.

Now, in the past, I have cried hysterically from happiness. I have laughed uncontrollably out of immense anger. And I have been so overly tired that I was unable to sleep.

But as the red-vested cashier asked the usual,
How are you today?

I responded,
Fine, thanks.

And somehow
I even managed to smile.

Currently Listening To:
Twenty One Pilots, "Stressed Out"

Track Forty

There are days I spill coffee
all over the passenger seat before 7 a.m.

Days I forget to pay bills
or respond to wedding invitations.

Days I am overwhelmingly sad
for reasons I cannot pinpoint.

Days I will no doubt attempt to pull
a door clearly marked *Push*.

Most days I find myself stumbling
over flat surfaces and expectations.

Yet, I know you will love me the same,
and that alone makes my daily
missteps less catastrophic.

Eternally Grateful,
Your Hot Mess

Currently Listening To:
Sublime, "Waiting for My Ruca"

Track Forty One

A message from the Universe appeared
in the form of a handwritten note taped
to the wall of a nail salon.

We are not responsible for your loss.

I knew the makeshift sign simply forewarned if I
left behind one of my possessions it was my fault,
not theirs. Yet, I took it to mean more, as if the
world was shaking me awake.

I need to stop making excuses.

I need to stop placing blame. I need to stop
renaming the decisions I've made as *mistakes* just
because I wish I could take them back.

Currently Listening To:
Jay Z feat. Justin Timberlake, "Holy Grail"

Track Forty Two

I never wanted to help you
with your problems
because I am selfish.

I knew if I were to let you go,
that alone would solve
every single issue in your life,
and I just wasn't ready
to leave you yet.

Currently Listening To:
Rita Ora, "Been Lying"

Track Forty Three

See you later, Cuz.

The last words my cousin ever said to me.

Last words.
What an unusual concept.

We rarely know they are the last
as they leave lips.

Though it was a dark time,
I am certain she believed
in her last words to me.

I am certain she believed
there would be another day.

Her last words were a promise.

And though, yes, we will never
see each other again in the physical,
I do believe I see my cousin all around me.

In dusty Emerson books
and in old Broadway ticket stubs.

In magazines we used to thumb through.

In her mother's laugh.
In an eye roll after hearing
her father's latest joke.
In a drive by a lake.
In yellowed photographs.
In the steep hill of her front lawn.

In shopping for CDs
and cheesy Sandra Bullock movies.

In ponytails and black hoodies.
In the title song from *Rent*.

In sushi dinners in New York City.

In Christmas mornings
and sarcastic remarks.

In an order of buffalo fries (*extra spicy*).

In Goo Goo Dolls song lyrics.

And most importantly, in my heart.

I use my words as a vessel to reach her.
To stay connected to her.
To keep her connected to us.
To hold up my end of our promise.

I will see you later, Cuz.

Currently *Listening To:*
Cast of Rent, *"Seasons of Love"*

Track Forty Four

The sand beneath my feet
    belongs to September now.
The salt air I inhale
    belongs to September now.
The crashing waves
    belong to September now.

August can have
my yesterdays;
my tomorrows
    belong to September now.

And my heart
    belongs to September now.

Currently Listening To:
Don Henley, "The Boys of Summer"

Track Forty Five

Dedicated to Kellie.

Sisters can have very little in common. No shared interests or friends or aspirations. The most my sister and I have in common most days are our blue eyes, parents, and my clothes.

Yet, we are tethered together, unfailingly.

It's one thing to have a support system in your life to cheer you on during the instances when everyone is rooting for you. However, it's another thing entirely to look back in your darkest moments and still see them standing in your corner, encouraging you to stay in the ring and FIGHT, when the odds aren't in your favor and all you want to do is throw in the towel.

Not many people in this life will be on your side even when they aren't on your side. Even less who momentarily will slam doors out of frustration but never actually lock you out.

Unconditional love; the definition of *sister*.

Currently Listening To:
Irving Berlin, "Sisters"

Track Forty Six

Packing up your belongings means nothing
if you can't box up your heart, scribble *fragile*
along the side, and take it with you, too.

It's hard to walk away, even if you know
in your heart of hearts it's necessary.
Even if your feet can't do the job
and you find yourself crawling on
your hands and knees away
from a toxic situation,

      be proud of yourself.

You are removing yourself
to better yourself
and you will stand
on your own two feet
again eventually.

So crawl, walk, or run;
      the *how* doesn't matter.
      Your new life is waiting for you.

Currently Listening To:
Eric Church, "Give Me Back My Hometown"

Track Forty Seven

This drugstore lipstick
is doing a poor job at covering
my chapped, bitten lips.

My sunglasses
are doing their best to hide
the dark circles surrounding my light eyes.

Would the wind feel this cold today
if you were still here?

I think back to the last real day we spent together;
there was nothing special about it. It was rushed,
and I remember the coffee tasting bitter. It's only
special now because it was our last.

Though I wish we had traded
everlasting last words, we didn't.
And we won't.

However, now when I have a cup
of bad coffee, it will taste less bitter
and more sweet. I will smile and savor it,
like the last real day we shared together.

Currently Listening To:
Lea Michele, "If You Say So"

Track Forty Eight

I was the kind of kid
who would step on ants
and then ask my mother
if their family
would miss them.

When I was ten,
I begged my parents
for a typewriter
and then had my father
show me how to
draft a professional résumé.

When I was eleven,
I coerced my siblings
and cousins
to perform skits
and lip-synch in music videos
I filmed with
the family camcorder.

When I was thirteen,
I would spend hours
after school writing
original stories
using the characters
from *Buffy the Vampire Slayer*

and the members of
the Backstreet Boys.
I had no idea
it was called
fan fiction at the time.

I was a witch
for Halloween six times;
not because
I lacked creativity,
but because
I desperately wanted
to be a witch.
Like, *for real.*

One day,
my uncle looked at me
and said,
You're a lonely soul, man.
It's possible,
I suppose.

I studied English
in a Catholic women's college
and, for my senior thesis,
rewrote *Alice in Wonderland*
from the White Rabbit's perspective.

I also explored in writing
the idea of Anna Karenina

being pushed under the carriage
of that passing train
against her will.

My professor told me
I didn't listen to
the essay instructions.

I got the paper back
and saw that I earned an A anyway
with a note saying,

Alicia, though you blatantly
ignored the prompt, after reading
this succinct conspiracy theory,
I can see the original essay topic
would have bored you.
Does your brain
ever slow down?

No.

Currently Listening To:
Cage the Elephant, "In One Ear"

Track Forty Nine

I love the way your tongue curls when
you are about to sneeze. I love that you don't
sit on the same side of the booth as me when
we are out to dinner. I love how you pretend
to notice my manicure.

And I love that I cannot
define the word *love*
without saying your name.

Anytime I am anywhere,
I wish you were beside me
because I am unable to separate
my life from yours.

Which leads me to believe you are my life,
and my life is you;

they are one and the same.

Currently Listening To:
Cast of Wicked, *"For Good"*

Track Fifty

The shore is always forgiving of the sea,
though they merge together
time and time again only to part.

The sea always returns to kiss the shore,
for both hold the innate understanding
that one cannot exist without the other.

We forgive each other for the very same reason.

Currently Listening To:
Emeli Sandé, "Read All About It (Part III)"

 Track Fifty One

I wear my yesterdays.

Yesterday's hair.
Yesterday's clothes.
Yesterday's makeup.

You.

My yesterdays are familiar but each day they
become more wrinkled, worn, and stained
and bring me less comfort. My past is
beginning to feel tight around my neck—*itchy.*

I like to believe I am outgrowing who I was
and what I needed when I was that person.

I like to think I will shed all of this,
even the skin you've touched.

It's nice to think about.

Currently Listening To:
Ingrid Michaelson, "Hell No"

Track Fifty Two

It's commonplace
to ramble off *I lost myself,*
when you go off course.

It's the perfect excuse,
one that allows you to admit fault
while simultaneously remaining the victim.

I admit I've even said it
after I fucked up
beyond a simple apology
and had to look my
collateral damage in the eyes.

Is that bullshit though?
Did I lose myself or just lose focus?
Did I become selfish,
even but for a moment,
and destroy something?

Perhaps we give so much of ourselves
away that we feel like essential pieces
of ourselves go missing.

We give ourselves away
to our past regrets and present aspirations,
to missed opportunities and everyday miracles,

to lovers and ex-lovers,
to harsh realities and unattainable daydreams,
to lost childhoods and ill-prepared adulthoods,
to flat tires and missed trains,
to friends and enemies,
to happy birthdays and hungover mornings,
to families and their fallen faces
when we let them down,
to fall festivities,
winter wonderlands,
sprung springs,
and summer suns.

I do not believe we lose ourselves.

I'd like to think we would never lose
something so precious if we could help it.

That, my friends,
I think life steals from us
from time to time.

Currently Listening To:
Mumford & Sons, "Little Lion Man"

Track Fifty Three

My brain is

   a l l
     o v e r
         the   place.

Grief will do that to you.

Today I sat in my car in my own driveway
for twenty minutes staring blankly
at my glove compartment.

My mind d r i f t e d o f f.

Grief will do that to you.

I found myself wondering why we still call this
thing a "glove compartment" when no one keeps
driving gloves, or any gloves for that matter, in
there anymore.

As a society, we are always talking about
progression. We are renaming TV stations and
street names—but can't rename this storage box
within our cars.

Don't fix what ain't broken, I guess.

Something broke me, and I need to be fixed.

Grief will do that to you.

What else would we call it?

Crumpled tissue holder.
Registration and insurance safe.

I question everything now,
even things that don't matter.

Grief will do that to you.

Currently Listening To:
Lynyrd Skynyrd, "Free Bird"

Track Fifty Four

One daybreak I woke to the aftermath of a surprise snowstorm. It was one of those storms that visit overnight when you least expect it, like in the middle of March even though the weather has warmed and you've stopped wearing a coat.

There was a lot of snow,
but the plows had arrived already.

I guess it wasn't as unexpected as I thought.

I got in my car and began my commute to work. It takes me through a park. That morning the park was blanketed in virgin snow. The bare trees wore the flakes like diamond earrings.

Everything was clean and beautiful,
white and pure.

It reminded me of snow days spent home from school. It reminded me of the fifteen minutes it took to suit up before going outside. It reminded me of snow angels and snow-adorned railroad tracks. It reminded me of the chill felt when ice would sneak inside my glove and shock my wrist. It reminded me of my mother laying our wet clothes on the radiators to dry.

I urged myself to pull over and take a picture of the beauty. That's how much the vision moved me. I wanted to stop and capture the scene; but I didn't. I was already driving too slow to make it to work on time so I just kept driving. The adult in me had won over my inner child. I promised myself I would take a picture on my ride back home—back through the same park.

As I sat at my desk that day, the temperature crept up and I watched the snow melt. I felt sad. By the time I was driving back through the park, everything was brown and dry again—litter was exposed—all the beauty had melted away. I should have stopped all of three seconds to take that damn picture. Who knows if I will see a winter wonderland like that again in my lifetime.

Thirty years old and I still think a moment will wait for me to catch up.

Currently Listening To:
Albert Hammond Jr., "Feed Me Jack"

Track Fifty Five

I spent a lot of my early twenties
making mistakes;
really bad ones.

The light of day was not my friend;
I was tired of how it illuminated my missteps.

I began plucking away at my blessings
like stars from the sky
just so my world could go black.

Enlightenment was something
I bumped into in the dark,
like a corner of a table or lamp.

Isolating yourself
does not make you unique,
it makes you a coward,
too afraid or ashamed
to show up for your own life.

I decided a long time ago
to stop exclusively chasing
my visions just when
my head was on a pillow.

I decided a long time ago
to be better off in the daylight.

To do better,
to be better,
to make other
things better.

My whole damn life
is my passion project.

You think I have big hair;
you should see my dreams.

Currently Listening To:
Jordin Sparks, "This Is My Now"

Track Fifty Six

*What is the difference between Earth
and the World?* I asked my fourth grade
teacher whose name escapes me.

She seemed to be using
the terms interchangeably.

*Since, right now,
humans only live
here on Earth,
the two words mean
the same thing,*
she answered.

As years went on, I found the two words to be
vastly different. Earth is the planet we inhabit,
yes, but the World is a unique plane of existence
to each person. As we plant roots and find love
and birth babies and become regulars at coffee
shops and restaurants, *the World* quickly
becomes *Our World*; mini colonies.

I've found that certain worlds can become as
narrow as hallways; and these passages I walk
through, the worlds I know, can
begin to feel constrictive.

The truth is, I've outgrown many worlds on Planet Earth, only to begin again. *Earth* provides the air we need to fill our lungs, but *Our Worlds* give us every reason to breathe deep. We must not take anything for granted on the exhale.

Currently Listening To:
Andy Grammer, "Back Home"

Track Fifty Seven

This mirror holds all my secrets;
my hopes and fears are mixed
with the toothpaste spatter
I keep forgetting to wipe away.

It sees me at my most vulnerable,
crusty eyed and naked face.

I am forced to face it each day.

You do not have it all together,
I write in the steam,
knowing it will disappear.

I realize that this may be
the most honest I will be all day.

Currently Listening To:
Mike Posner, "Be As You Are"

Track Fifty Eight

Your teeth will begin to chatter.
Your fingertips will turn blue.
Your lips will chap and your eyes will tear.

You will wonder why
you just can't shake
that penetrating chill
within your bones.

It is because
my warmth
left your heart.

Currently Listening To:
ZZ Ward, "365 Days"

Track Fifty Nine

I want a busy kitchen, with small fingerprint smudges on the refrigerator door. I want a crowded bed where all nightmares disappear. I want to jump in a cold pool or ocean and still smile. I want early Christmas mornings, with stockings held by the chimney with care and little voices whispering *Santa came!* I want to be a thirty-something-year-old in a pointy cardboard birthday hat. I want my homemade chicken noodle soup to cure colds and my Band-Aid kisses to heal knee scrapes. I want to freeze moments in cement. I want to learn to swim again, skip through sprinklers again, welcome the tooth fairy again, and make sand castles again. I want to believe in magic again.

I want to be born again.

Currently Listening To:
Waitress *the Musical, "Everything Changes"*

Track Sixty

The letters behind the cursor are already in the
past. That's how fast it all happens. A finite twenty-six
letters create an infinite trail of breadcrumbs
that lead to different moments that lead to who
I was just a moment before.

I am no longer the person
I was just a twinkling ago.

The changes are so minute,
but they are there—
you may think you remain
the same person you were

a day ago,
   an hour ago,
      a page ago,
         a   line   break   ago,

but you are not.

Currently Listening To:
Wrabel, "11 Blocks"

Track Sixty One

Maybe you've gone through something
no one should have to go through
at such a young age.

Maybe you know the pain
of a loss so deep,
your marrow aches.

Not many know the anguish felt in

growing older than your older sister.
Having her laugh stolen from you
in the middle of a joke.
Talking in past tense.

Everything will be in
past tense from now on.

Maybe you know what it is like
to wake up from slumber,
covered in your own tears.

Maybe each pump of your heart hurts
your chest, but your heart pumps, even still.

This pain is reminding you
that you are alive.

There is an empowerment
uncorked in grief.

Your life will never be the same, ever,
so you can never be the same, ever.

Pain will make you stronger,
but it will make you a lot
of other things first.

Maybe at its worst,
it will cripple you;

but, maybe,
at its best,
it will become
your superpower.

Currently Listening To:
Queen, "We Are the Champions"

Track Sixty Two

Growth or a change
in my perspective
will turn some people off,
turn some people away.

This doesn't mean
I am growing in the wrong direction.
It's important to remember
no one needs to be in my corner
as long as I am in my corner.
No one needs to witness my comeback;
what matters is I come back.

This is not a classic underdog story;
I am not a phoenix.
I did not rise from the ashes—
I crawled out from under the soot,

fingernails cracked,
palms bloody,
face muddy.

I told you I'd be okay one day.
Today is that day.

Currently Listening To:
Ben Rector, "Make Something Beautiful"

Track Sixty Three

If you ever left,
          in rhyme.

The wind would still come
   and the chimes would still play.
The sun would still rise
   and the moon would end the day.
The waves would still crash
   and the gulls would still caw.

But I,
   I wouldn't be the same.
   Not at all.

Currently Listening To:
Taylor Swift, "All Too Well"

Track Sixty Four

I have begun measuring life
not just in numbers
and years
but in sunsets and
trees blossoming and
brilliant views.

You cannot calculate my growth by the notches
etched in the molding of my bedroom wall. You
cannot understand my scars by the nicks on my
knees and elbows. You cannot grasp my
metamorphosis by the skin I've shed or
the baby teeth I've lost.

It cannot be determined in anything I've lost or
in what's marred me. It can only be quantified in
what remains, in what withstood every storm
and every disruption of my heart.

You can see my growth simply by the fact that I
am still standing here, believing that this world
is still an inherently good place to laugh, to hurt,
to love, to lose, to exist.

Currently Listening To:
Adele, "River Lea"

Track Sixty Five

EWR to UAU

You know something bad happened last night, but you don't pry. You figure I'll bring it up when I'm ready. We board the flight. We take off. I remember mumbling something to you about how I never sleep on planes (granted, I haven't slept in my own bed in some time, either). Suddenly, my body shuts down and I slump onto your shoulder. Sleep found me before 30,000 feet. I wake a bit startled, a bit surprised, and for the first time in weeks (or has it been years?), a bit rested. *My mind was finally able to rest, knowing I was flying far away from here.* You offer me your neck pillow and a smile.

Currently Listening To:
Bruno Mars, "It Will Rain"

Track Sixty Six

I am under construction. Not many people like to admit that, but everyone is always in the process of becoming something else. No one is ever really finished—constructed and complete.

I am starting to sleep at a normal hour again. *So that probably means I am healing.* Sleep is the first thing to leave you after something like this. Sanity follows soon after. The loss of one is definitely directly related to the loss of the other.

I still have some trouble getting out of bed come morning, but I learned what matters most is getting out of bed at all. I've read about people who were so sad, they stayed in bed all day. That alone motivated me to want to get up, even if I just moved to the couch. *The couch is not the bed.*

A lot of what I knew left with you, and that made me tired. Ask any school-aged child, learning new things at times can be frustrating and draining. It hasn't been a fluid progression of bad to better, but my repaired days have begun to outnumber my damaged ones.

Currently Listening To:
Ruth B, "Lost Boy"

Track Sixty Seven

I used to love hotel rooms.
Now, the sheets feel stiff
and the unacquainted features
of the room do not hold the same allure.

The white bedding
doesn't smell like the wet towel
you absentmindedly left on our bed.

The pillowcases
don't hold the distinct scent
of your raven hair.

The air doesn't smell
like your cologne.

The closet
holds a dripping iron
but your sneakers are nowhere to be found.

The room service I ordered
doesn't include you,
sipping coffee across from me,
asking me about my day.

Currently Listening To:
Lifehouse, "You and Me"

Track Sixty Eight

To the guy who fell asleep on the couch:

We're private; many can't understand why we
don't share every second of our lives with the
masses. Many get excited to have a wedding,
and wear the pretty dress, and put on the
expensive rings; but that one day in the scheme
of "forever" that is celebrated annually doesn't
really matter. The stuff to really celebrate comes
after that day. Choosing to stay together. To
work on things. I've got to be one of the most
difficult people to love and remain in love with;
I'm sometimes selfish and my chaotic thoughts
translate into the mess I leave around our house.
I'm independent in most aspects of my life but
totally dependent when it comes to you.
Without you, I'd fall apart. Some time ago,
I decided on forever, and I am so very
fortunate you did, too.

Currently Listening To:
Jason Mraz, "I Won't Give Up"

Track Sixty Nine

Memories are mere echoes
of the actual occurrence.
Distorted in the reverberation.
Romanticized in the ricochet.

My ghost towns were crowded
for such a long time.
You don't haunt me anymore.
Memory lane is just another street
I turn left at on my way to
the grocery store now.

I prefer it this way.

Currently Listening To:
Beyoncé, "Sorry"

Track Seventy

Scraped knees. Black eyes. Tears.

This is all pain we can see. Pain we can aid.
Pain that will heal if we tend and mend.

Then, there is *that other pain.*

The pain so embedded into our being, so deep,
that it fuses to our existence and mixes with our
bloodstream. It doesn't just become a part of us,
it becomes who we are.

It's that other pain you can't see that never
really heals, not fully anyway. It's also the pain
that gives us a higher purpose. The kind of pain
that will turn you into a warrior.

Those mascara streaks are your war paint;
wear them proudly.

Currently Listening To:
Big Sean, "Deep"

Track Seventy One

I am too focused on my next move to worry
about what everyone on earth is doing next. I
don't need to beat down who I was yesterday, or
anyone else for that matter, to grow. I don't take
advantage of the disadvantages of others. I
refuse to race against time, other women, or
men. I can only reach my next level,
not anyone else's.

I compete with my own benchmarks,
my own comfort zones,
my own inner strength,
and my own voice.

Currently Listening To:
Tim McGraw, "Humble and Kind"

Track Seventy Two

I have demanded to speak to God directly three
times. Three times in three decades is not a lot,
I'd say. I found Him the other night, in a
different place than I found Him last.

The first time I found Him wading within
the crests of waves of water too cold to swim.
The second time, I found Him sleeping
inside the thread count of my beloved's sheets.

This time I found Him stitched into
the song of my mother's wind chimes.

I had gone outside to catch my breath.

Outside there is more air,
enough air to save me.

I had my heartbreak,
I had my breakdown,
now I needed my breakthrough.

At that very moment,
the unmistakable wind that bridged seasons
blew through my unwashed hair
and the trees and the metal cylinders
my mother attached to their branches
and He sang to me.

His melody calmed me
and I was able to hear the crickets
and my family conversing at the dinner table
and the static from my father's record player
over the pounding in my head and heart again.

I was brought out of the past
and placed into the present.

That's the thing about faith;
if you are looking,
you will find it;

if you need it,
you will find it;

if you believe,
you will find it.

Currently Listening To:
Christina Grimmie, "I Bet You Don't Curse God"

Track Seventy Three

Yesterday was a good day. I woke up easy, slow.
The smell from the air conditioner in my
window welcomed me like the warm
aroma of coffee brewing.

Yesterday was a good day. The forecast called for
rain, but the sun shined all day. I read a book in
my hammock. The battery in my phone lasted an
impressive seven hours. The clothes I ordered
got delivered and everything fit perfectly.

Yesterday was a good day. The barista made my
latte perfectly and there was no line at the
pharmacy. There were no shadows, no ominous
clouds, and three of my favorite songs played in
a row on the radio.

Yesterday was a good day
even though you didn't come back.

My heart noticed the shift
and smiled.

Currently Listening To:
Maren Morris, "Rich"

Track Seventy Four

I am the most put-together broken person you will ever come across; with hairline fractures so fine, my skin remains smooth to the touch. I see I am shattered; broken shards placed together and called art, *a mosaicked woman.*

Are you having another one of your dark days?
My father asks.

Days in a daze become weeks of being weak. Months become moths that eat holes into my favorite moments.

There was a time I laughed more, was more lighthearted and whimsical. There was a time I smiled in more than just pictures. There was once a time I at least attempted to end pieces on high notes.

I'll get back there.
See? A high note.

Currently Listening To:
Ben Rector, "Fear"

Track Seventy Five

The ocean resides outside where my parents
stay. I breathe in deep. I like the smell of
summer, but the thought of winter
keeps me warm.

December was when you loved me last. Your
mind shifted from me before your heart left. The
crashing waves sound like the dishes I threw
against the wall that night.

If I am broken, the plates we eat
on should be broken, too.

Seagulls caw in the distance,
and I am tired.

Tired of tirelessly crying
over the same old bullshit story.

I love you,
but not right now.

I want you,
but not right now.

The humidity in the air has caused
my footprints to create a trail on the tile.

Now my mother is going to be able to tell
I have been walking in circles.

I've always preferred hardwood floors
but being so close to the ocean doesn't allow it.
The salt in the air can cause
structural damage to the wood;
any beach kid knows this.

I've always preferred you over any other man
but being so close to you doesn't allow it.
The hurt in the air can cause
structural damage to my heart;
any brokenhearted woman knows this.

Currently Listening To:
Carrie Underwood, "Little Toy Guns"

Track Seventy Six

Darkness is like a sleeping bear—
it should not be poked, provoked.

Still, too many I know are hunting
down nightmares, pissing away the same
time life allots to chase dreams.

I can't take it anymore, honestly,
all this darkness.

I have lost my voice
trying to convince people I love
of their own potential.

I have been the collateral damage
to a number of life tragedies
that were not directly my own.

I've swept up messes I haven't created
and dried tears I haven't cried.
I've aged just by witnessing others lose years.

Self-destruction destroys
more than just the individual.

Currently Listening To:
Christina Perri, "Butterfly"

Track Seventy Seven

Let's be clear. I did not accidently step into my
life. I loved and worked every single day. A good
thing happening to a good person is not luck.
Just like how a bad thing happening to a bad person
is not bad luck. Sometimes, it's just life. I've
been hurt. I've cried into my pillow. I've
experienced loss. I have been overlooked and
underestimated more times than I'd like to
admit. I have experienced moments
of good fortune.

Life is all about balance;
I am a firm believer that you get
what you give in this world.

Yes, I am loved—
because I love.
Yes, I am taken care of—
because I take care of others.
Yes, I have friends—
because I am a friend.

I am not going to apologize for my life,
just like how life did not apologize
to me when things weren't going my way.

Currently Listening To:
Maren Morris, "Second Wind"

Track Seventy Eight

I hollowed out my memory;
to make room for what's to come.

I scooped out the gunk;
the letdowns, the heartache,
and left the happiness.

Yet, I was no longer myself;
unbalanced.

Maybe I was meant to be sad, I thought.

I plopped back in the painful
and scooped out the happiness;
the weddings, the graduations,
the moments I laughed until I cried.

Once again I found myself unstable.

We need both.
We need the good
and the bad
to be who we are.

For better or worse, we need both.

Currently Listening To:
Ingrid Michaelson, "Drink You Gone"

Track Seventy Nine

Your face jolted me from sleep.

The details do not matter,
because you no longer matter.

I startled the man sleeping next to me;
the man who matters.

What is it? he asked, concerned.
Nothing. It was just a nightmare.

I wasn't lying.

Currently Listening To:
Billy Currington, "It Don't Hurt Like It Used To"

Track  Eighty

I believe in what destroyed me.
I believe it needed to destroy me.
My pain is not in vain.

What I went through
replaced my backbone,
once as brittle as a wishbone,
with a sword.

Currently Listening To:
Whitney Houston, "It's Not Right but It's Okay"

Track Eighty One

When I was leaving your funeral,
church bells sang announcing
another hour in my life,

another hour lived without you.

Birds chirped
and I heard a sprinkler
spraying water on grass
already too green for its own good.

It would have been a great day
if it wasn't already the worst day of my life.

Across from the church was a playground;
children swung on the swings,
in tune to the bells.

A child's eyes met mine;
they were warm, welcoming.

Not only was life still going on,
it was still smiling at me.

Currently Listening To:
Luke Bryan, "Drink a Beer"

Track Eighty Two

I do believe the sun will come out after each
storm, though no one knows how long one of
life's storms will last.

Could be a passing shower,
could be a yearlong monsoon.

You aren't a fictional green witch;
you will not melt if you get a little wet.

I would say *learn to dance in the rain*
but that's too much of a Goddamn cliché
these days; at the very least,
find the simple joy of jumping
in the puddles life creates.

Currently Listening To:
Gene Kelly, "Singin' in the Rain"

Track Eighty Three

Some things slow my world down
but nothing has truly
stopped it from spinning.

I don't give up;
even when I feel defeated
and proclaim,
I give up,
I never really do.

What I've been carrying quietly
on my shoulders for years
you wouldn't be able to hoist
onto your back for one day.

The loudest people in the room
aren't always the most heard,
the people crying the loudest
aren't always the most hurt.

Currently Listening To:
Christina Aguilera, "Fighter"

Track Eighty Four

I still miss you from time to time.

What's changed is how I've begun
to handle *the missing*.

I've learned that pain passes;
the missing, it passes.

Much like a dizzy spell,
I just have to wait until my vision
and mind clear and the aching clears, too.

That's how I healed.

I woke up every day,
cried or didn't cry,
regained my balance,
and went the hell on with my day,

which eventually turned into me
getting the hell on with my life.

Currently Listening To:
Gloria Gaynor, "I Will Survive"

Track  Eighty Five

If you are feeling lost,
helpless,
down,
sad,
angry,
betrayed,
you name it,

you can rise from it,
you can create from it,
you can grow from it.

I am living proof
the most turbulent year of one's life
could also turn out to be
the greatest, more rewarding year, too.

Currently Listening To:
Florida Georgia Line, "May We All"

Track Eighty Six

Some weekend mornings in my new home,
I wake up to the bark of the dog in the
connecting yard. When I do, for a second, I
believe it's the bark of my family dog.

The dog that still sleeps an hour away in the
house where I grew up, with the family I see far
less than I wish. The dog we've had since I was
thirteen years old. The aging dog who spends
more time with my parents than I do.

Now, I know it is not him I hear; but for a
moment I am back in my old bedroom, in the
busy home where I shared a wall, computer, and
clothes with my sister and a bathroom with four
other people. I am back, hearing pots clanging
and sauce simmering in my mother's kitchen.

Then, I fully awake, and I am in my new home.
Though I wake alone in a quiet house some
mornings, I find comfort in the notion of *home*.
You don't have to remember to take Home with
you when you move on; you carry Home in your
heart, and on some really lucky days, Home
visits you through the bark of a stranger's pet.

Currently Listening To:
Crosby, Stills, Nash & Young, "Our House"

Track Eighty Seven

I accomplished everything in my life
in spite of you, not because of you.

You can't take my happiness from me anymore,
because you are no longer the underlying reason.
You can't take something back from someone
you never even held in your own two hands
in the first place.

You do not hold my happiness.
You do not own my happiness.
I manifest my own happiness.

I came this far on a broken heart—
functioning at maybe, on a good day,
forty percent efficiency.

I think you should be nervous
about what I will accomplish once I heal.

The mountains I'll move.
The miles I'll cover.
The skin I'll get under.

Currently Listening To:
Sia, "Alive"

Track Eighty Eight

I don't belong here;
I'm out of sync with what's around me.
My heart doesn't belong here;
it beats out of time,
like a drum in the wrong song.
Oh, how I wish for a breeze to find me;

I'd scatter like confetti
into the air,
ending up in one million
different places at once.

What a magical escape.

Currently Listening To:
Ryn Weaver, "Pierre"

Track Eighty Nine

He looks in my eyes and he knows he's lost me.
Not forever but for the next few hours.

My stare is unfocused;
the sadness simmering inside of me
has boiled to the surface.

I feel every organ that matters:
my lungs, my heart, my brain.

They have become heavy,
weighing me down in bed.

He looks in my eyes and knows
I'll be back soon enough;
so he rests beside me,
making sure he's the first thing
I will see when my heart wakes up again.

Currently Listening To:
Miranda Lambert, "Runnin' Just in Case"

Track Ninety

I find myself singing
to the rhythm of your breathing.

You know the doors
to all four chambers of my heart.

You know which creak
and which open freely.

Most importantly, you know
how to pry open the jammed doors
so many others confused for locked.

You push with all your might,
and I let you in.

Currently Listening To:
Train, "Meet Virginia"

Track Ninety One

Doors remain ajar as long as two people allow.
Once someone makes the decision to leave,
the ajar door slams shut right behind them
with the wind and the letdowns.

You cannot reenter once this happens.
You cannot reenter that life ever again.

You're no longer an invited guest,
you are an intruder.

Currently Listening To:
The Lumineers, "Stubborn Love"

Track Ninety Two

Gathering rays, seashells, and memories.
I collect my thoughts along the seashore.

I place one close to my ear.
I listen intently.

Breathe in, breathe out,
you've made it to the other side.

Currently Listening To:
The Band Perry, "Comeback Kid"

side B
the remixes

Track One

This is dedicated to the man who saved me.

He didn't save me from a car wreck;
my existence managed to swerve off the road,
creating a mangled mess even the
Jaws of Life couldn't tear through.

He didn't save me from fiery flames.
Quite the contrary, and perhaps
even a bit more frightening, the fire inside
of me had long burned out.

He didn't save me from drowning,
at least not in the literal sense.
I can swim just fine and still the rip currents
of life took me under, and I began
to flounder in my own tears.

Simply, this is dedicated to the man who saved
me from the biggest catastrophe of all: *myself.*

Currently Listening To:
The Fray, "How to Save a Life"

Track Two

~~You~~ ~~always want one more day.~~
~~You always~~ ~~want~~ ~~one more picture~~
~~as the old ones begin to fade.~~
~~You always want that one final hug~~
~~to have lasted just~~ ~~a~~ ~~tad longer.~~
~~You always want the fondness~~
~~of the remember whens~~
~~to outnumber the might have beens.~~
~~You want more years, more months,~~
~~more weeks, more days,~~
~~more minutes, and more~~ ~~seconds~~~~.~~
~~You want the~~ *happily ever after*
~~you always thought you deserved,~~
~~but the only thing actually promised~~
in this life ~~is uncertainty.~~

Currently Listening To:
Frank Sinatra, "The Second Time Around"

Track Three

I c o m b through my memories
with more
care than I do my hair.

I'm told the key is to preserve the root.

Still, I have difficult remembering things

I recall second natures

in

b
a
r
r
a
s
,

never wholes.

I flip through photo albums
and see my likeness in someone
I can't manage to recognize anymore,
even when I squint.

~~She shares my fingerprints.~~
~~They tell me it's me.~~

~~It's as if I am wearing~~
~~hand-me-down memories~~
~~from a~~ life ~~that doesn't fit quite right.~~

~~They were~~ a gift
~~so squeeze into them.~~

~~I experience that familiar itch of frustration~~
~~as I struggle to name the girl in the photo.~~

~~Imagine the anguish felt~~
~~by having your very own existence~~
~~on the tip of your tongue.~~

Currently Listening To:
Drake, "You & the 6"

Track Four

Yeah, she's beautiful.
Anyone with decent eyesight can tell you that.

That's not why I love her.

I love her when she is putting on her makeup,
sitting on the bathroom counter.

I love her when she makes me order
the Chinese or pizza
but constantly whispers the order
into my ear because she is convinced
I'll mess it up.

I love her when we are walking
and she trips over nothing on the sidewalk
and keeps talking, not missing a beat,
like it just didn't happen.

I love her when we are packing the car
for a trip and she hands me seven bags.

I love her when she is curled up
on our couch wearing my shirt.

I love her after her first sip of coffee
or her last sip of wine.

~~I love her when she first gets out of the shower~~
~~in the~~ (summer) ~~and I see her vivid tan lines.~~

~~I love her when she steals the covers all night~~
~~and then, come morning,~~
~~blames me for turning on the fan.~~

~~I love her when we~~ (drive during) ~~the holidays,~~
~~her feet up on the dashboard,~~
~~sipping hot chocolate and~~
~~looking at~~ (Christmas) ~~lights.~~

Currently Listening To:
Bing Crosby, "White Christmas"

Track Five

~~She jumped from one happiness~~
~~to the next.~~ *~~(You're the only one.)~~*

~~They made her smile~~
~~(You're beautiful)~~
~~until they made her cry~~
~~(But I'm not looking to settle down.)~~

~~They broke~~ her heart *~~This isn't~~*
~~working anymore,)~~ ~~and her spirit~~
~~(But let's still be friends.)~~

~~Over and over again,~~
~~she trusted the~~ ~~f r a g m e n t s~~
~~of her soul with others~~
~~(I'd never hurt you like he did.)~~

~~She thought they could fix her.~~
~~Once they~~ inevitably abandoned her
~~(It's not you, it's me)~~ ~~she would end up~~
~~leaving with more of them than of herself.~~

~~And this is how a person's own reflection~~
~~can become unrecognizable.~~

Currently Listening To:
Anna Nalick, "Breathe (2 AM)"

Track Six

~~The strongest people I know~~
~~have been overtaken by their~~ weaknesses
~~They know what it's like to lose control.~~
~~The strongest people I know~~
~~have cried in the shower and in their car.~~
~~They know loss and guilt all too well.~~
~~The strongest people I know~~ are ~~n't bulletproof.~~
~~They have felt the searing pain of life's shots.~~
The strongest ~~people I know~~
~~make the decision every day to wake up~~
~~and place their two feet on the ground~~
~~even though they know the~~ monsters ~~beneath~~
~~their bed will grab at their ankles.~~

~~The strongest people~~ I know
~~are not strong by definition, at all.~~

~~They are mistake-makers.~~
They are mess-creators.
~~They are survivors.~~

Currently Listening To:
8 Mile *motion picture,* "Final Battle"

Track Seven

To Whom It May Concern:

Drive away. You don't live here anymore.

You are not home free if you are still calling this place Home. Check your mirrors. *Images are closer than they appear and not as pretty as they seem.* Those rose-colored sunglasses of yours are playing tricks on your eyes. This nostalgic route is messing with your heart. That familiar song on the radio has penetrated your mind.

Honestly, I hope you don't spend one minute missing me. Missing this. You will heal as long as you don't turn around. *Ever.* Sometimes even a glance into the past can kill you.

Sincerely,
The Girl You Used to Be

Currently Listening To:
The Airborne Toxic Event, "Sometime Around Midnight"

Track Eight

~~She lost herself.~~

~~I'm talking~~ *~~down-the-rabbit-hole-free-fall~~* ~~like the little blonde girl in that~~ book ~~she read once. She was so far gone, even her own shadow kicked her when she was down. Friends and family would tell her she would be~~ her *old* ~~self in no time flat.~~

~~You'll find yourself again,~~ ~~they would say. They would~~ promise ~~her this in hopes she would find comfort in the possibility. They made it seem like a blessing. To her, the idea~~ of ~~becoming herself again felt more like a curse. Why would she purposely go hunting for that girl just to feel all the pain she had once felt?~~

~~Why? If that meant having the memories, mistakes, and regrets find her again, too? No, she didn't want to become her~~ *~~old self~~* ~~again.~~

~~If she survived her latest mis~~adventure ~~she vowed to become someone entirely new.~~

Currently Listening To:
Passenger, "Scare Away the Dark"

Track Nine

The first time my heart broke, I thought back to
the day in my childhood when a piece of glass went
through my finger after an ill-fated cartwheel.

I was eleven years old.

My mother and I were in our bathroom cleaning
up the wound. She dribbled peroxide onto the cut.
It fizzed and burned; I winced at the pain.

It needs to burn so you know it's healing,
she explained.

That small exchange during my adolescence helped
me learn to appreciate the pain pulsating from my
broken heart. In spite of the severity of my wound,
I knew the healing process had already begun.

Currently Listening To:
Melanie Safka, "Look What They've Done to My Song, Ma"

Track Ten

~~I had become accustomed to using moving boxes~~
~~as makeshift~~ (coffee) ~~tables. I was never in one place~~
~~for too long and always in my car longer than any~~
~~bed, but there was an anomaly~~ (in that last) ~~drive.~~

~~It was one of those special car rides where every~~
~~song on the radio was~~ (one of my favorite)~~s. The~~
~~road was open and smooth, freshly paved.~~

~~And the~~ (thing is,) ~~I wasn't driving anywhere new.~~
~~For once~~ (in my) (life,) ~~home had become a~~
~~singular destination for me.~~

~~I regained my soul through you.~~
~~I regained my soul through our consistency.~~

Currently Listening To:
The Verve, "Bitter Sweet Symphony"

Track Eleven

~~You~~ (can) ~~taste sorrow in salt tears and in the bitterness of spoiled words left in your mouth for far too long.~~

~~You can hear sorrow in a familiar~~ (song.) ~~You~~ (can) ~~hide sorrow behind closed doors and inside screams muffled by pillowcases.~~

~~You can stick to sorrow as if it were gum in your hair, too mangled to brush out, too jarring to chop off.~~

~~You can see sorrow in bloodshot eyes and shaky hands.~~

~~You can get lost in sorrow when it knocks your life off course with no detour signs to~~ (redirect you.)

~~Most importantly, you can be found in sorrow by becoming a different version of yourself, here, on the other side of tragedy.~~

Currently Listening To:
Amy Winehouse, "Tears Dry on Their Own"

Track Twelve

~~My *new beginnings* have often spawned from forced endings. With one of life's chapters being ripped from my hands before I even had time to dog-ear my favorite part.~~ For a very long time I ~~confused the notion of *a fresh start* with~~ walking toward distress instead of away from it.

~~Now, I relish the thought of getting to know the~~ unknown. ~~Getting to familiarize myself with the unfamiliar. Getting to start over smack dab in the middle of my life whenever I damn well please.~~

Currently Listening To:
Alessia Cara, "Here"

Track Thirteen

~~There has always been a d i s c o n n e c t~~
~~between me and the world around me;~~
(I never) felt (settled) ~~grounded.~~

~~Suddenly, it became so clear.~~
~~Perhaps I lost myself so often because~~
~~I found my sandy feet in a shore town.~~

(All my life) ~~my footprints were~~
~~repeatedly washed away by the tide,~~
~~as if I never existed there in the first place.~~

Currently Listening To:
Kacey Musgraves, "Good Ol' Boys Club"

Track Fourteen

~~Just because~~ (I don't) ~~trust you~~
~~doesn't~~ (mean) ~~I have trust issues.~~
~~Just because I won't commit~~ (to) ~~you~~
~~doesn't mean I have commitment issues.~~
~~Just b~~ (cause) ~~I watch what I eat~~
~~doesn't mean I have body image issues.~~
~~Just because people have left my life~~
~~doesn't mean I have abandonment issues.~~
~~Just because I yearn to grow and evolve~~
~~doesn't mean I have identity issues.~~

~~I know exactly who the~~ (hell) ~~I am.~~

Currently Listening To:
The Strokes, "Reptilia"

Track Fifteen

A picture never fully captures
the reasons behind why I want
to freeze the moment
in the first place.

It doesn't capture the distant
smell of a fireplace burning as
it's quietly overtaken by the
unmistakable aroma of low tide.
It doesn't capture the cleansing
scent of salt air entering my nostrils.
It doesn't capture the monstrous
howl of the wind whipping through
my hair or the pleasurable
sting of the sand in my eyes.

It doesn't capture the transformation
in the texture of the sand beneath
my feet as I approach the breakers.
It doesn't capture the unexpected warmth
of November's ocean as it reaches my ankles.

The lens of a camera cannot capture any of that,
my heart does.

Currently Listening To:
Snow Patrol, "Just Say Yes"

Track Sixteen

~~The~~ *~~new normal~~* is rarely ~~an easy adjustment and never truly feels, well, normal.~~

~~Let's be~~ honest.

~~Plan B~~ ~~is never preferred.~~
~~Detours and alternate routes~~
~~are never quite as scenic.~~

~~The darkness of being gifted a second chance~~
~~is that it means something went~~
~~wrong in the first place.~~

And yet,

I ~~would rather have a few speed bumps slow me~~
~~down, causing me to~~ spill ~~coffee on my dress, than~~
~~ever hand someone else the keys to~~ my life.

Currently Listening To:
The Growlers, "Naked Kids"

142

Track Seventeen

~~Sometimes you don't realize~~
you are h o l d i n g yourself
together ~~until~~

~~you~~
~~aren't~~
~~anymore.~~

~~Suddenly, you're not the same~~
~~person you thought you were~~
just ~~m o m e n t s before.~~

~~No.~~

~~You are not okay.~~
~~You are not~~ fine
~~But you will be.~~

~~When I say~~ *you will be okay,*
~~I do not mean you will wake up~~
one day ~~and be the same person~~
~~you were before the pain.~~

~~Pain changes a person.~~

~~But, you will discover a~~
~~new version of yourself.~~

143

~~One who has experienced the great sadness~~
~~that only follows a great loss.~~

~~One who knows the~~
~~value of a good cry.~~

~~One who knows that even after~~
~~the coldest of winters,~~
~~spring will still arrive.~~

Currently Listening To:
Lana Del Rey, "Radio"

Track Eighteen

~~We cleanse our palates as midnight resets our~~
~~lives. Clean slates always taste better when fizzy.~~
~~The unknown is easier digested when fizzy.~~

Currently Listening To:
Rufus Wainwright, "Hallelujah"

Track Nineteen

~~There are~~

~~lay~~
~~ers~~

~~to loving me.~~

~~In the beginning,~~ (I am quite) ~~easy to love.~~
~~My surface is smooth, my smiles tender.~~

~~But as time undresses,~~
~~my insides are revealed to be rough and ragged.~~
~~It will become awfully difficult to love me.~~
~~At times, borderline~~ (impossible)

~~Many have left, for people would rather~~
~~see a car accident unfold from afar,~~
~~than be the shotgun rider.~~

~~Until you.~~

~~Only you can see all you see, know all you know~~
~~about me, and still look at me like this.~~

Currently Listening To:
Lenka, "The Show"

Track Twenty

(My life) ~~ong person.~~
~~The man who~~ (will) ~~help~~
~~zip my dress every morning.~~

~~How do you do it?~~

~~You~~ (fix) ~~everything~~
~~time and time again~~
~~just by surviving~~
~~t h r o u g h t h e~~
~~moment with~~ (me.)

Currently Listening To:
Mat Kearney, "Ships in the Night"

Track Twenty One

If you are lucky enough to have a childhood friend, try your hardest to grow old with them. These friends are a unique, irreplaceable breed.

These friends lived through curfews and Polaroid pictures with you. These friends know your parents and siblings because they had to call your house first to speak with you. Your memories are not frozen in time on social media, but live on nonetheless.

Most importantly, they remember the person you were before the world got ahold of you, so they have this crazy ability to love you no matter what.

They are the living, breathing reflection of where you have been. And so, just when you think you've lost yourself for good, they are there to bring you face-to-face with your true self, simply by sharing a cup of coffee with them.

As your world grows and becomes larger and more complicated than your backyard, even if you establish a life elsewhere, I hope your childhood friends remain lifelong allies, because mine have saved my life on more than one occasion.

Currently Listening To:
Tim McGraw, "Meanwhile Back at Mama's"

Track Twenty Two

2015

I didn't just survive this year
I lived it.

I laughed, I cried,
I scribbled things in journals.
My heart broke, but kept ticking.
My passport earned a few new stamps.

I had fancy Saturdays
and lazy Sundays.

I dipped my toes in tropical seas.
I hiked mountains
and cheated on my diet.

I made my twenty-ninth
consecutive birthday wish.

Because of this, and so much more,
I will never settle on simply
surviving ever again.

I choose to live.

Currently Listening To:
Zac Brown Band, "Highway 20 Ride"

Track Twenty Three

I want you to know,
I love you the other 364 days, too.

All the commercially popular grand gestures in the world could never compete with the millions of everyday little things you have done, and continue to do, for me. You continue to love me when I am, by definition, unlovable. You continue to love me when I don't particularly love myself. You allow me to remain my quirky self in a world that prefers conformity. I can only hope I bring to you the same feeling of completeness and unconditional acceptance that you have given to me.

Love isn't about tangible things.
Love has always been about two people.

And since we are only allotted one life per person, I feel undeniably privileged and fortunate to get to spend my one lifetime with you.

Currently Listening To:
Blake Shelton, "Who Are You When I'm Not Looking"

Track Twenty Four

For the first time
in months,
I didn't wear a jacket
on Sunday.

I woke up and felt *different*.

Even before I cracked open my windows, allowing
what definitely resembled a spring breeze to creep
through and ruffle the loose papers on my dresser.
Even before I heard birds chirping and a seagull
cawing overhead. Even before the aroma of freshly
ground coffee entered my nostrils, smelling more
like a pleasure than a necessity. It was as if my soul
had thawed. I felt completely reinvigorated.
Instead of wearing one of my seventeen pairs of black
yoga pants I had been wearing since October, I opted
for an olive green maxi dress and a light cardigan.
Others felt the change, too. I noticed some girls in
flip-flops hopscotching through puddles
of melting snow.

Call it ridiculous, but there was an upswing in my
mood, just at the mere promise of spring.

Perhaps my decision to nix the jacket was a symbol
for change, not just in the weather, but within
myself.

~~I caught a glimpse of the girl I had been missing greatly the last couple of months. It was nice to see her again.~~

~~So Sunday, I sang along with the radio really loudly and unapologetically, I drank three mimosas before one o'clock, and I didn't wear a jacket.~~

Currently Listening To:
O.A.R., "Peace"

Track Twenty Five

I am never going to be the girl with the perfectly straightened hair or creased clothing. Even at my most put together, I'll look a bit d i s h e v e l e d.

My socks will never match, but no one will notice that except for my lover and airport security. At the most inopportune times, I'll have a run in my stocking or a runny nose.

I'll combine foods even a pregnant woman wouldn't crave. On way more than one occasion, my friends have said out loud, *I would not want to spend one minute in you head.*

I was always aware of what I encompassed. I have never tried to conform because I did not feel the pressure to do so *(thanks, Mom!)*. Yes, this self-assurance led to my grade school years being a living hell, but even then I recognized that time of my life as temporary.

I do not fear, nor am I ashamed of, myself.

As long as I am happy, it is my God-given right to be odd. To be my true self.

Currently Listening To:
Frank Sinatra, "My Way"

Track Twenty Six

~~The way you peer~~
~~into~~ (my depths)
~~with such ease,~~
~~my soul must~~
~~have a glass bottom.~~

(You) ~~embrace~~
~~my complexity~~
~~and bravely swim~~
~~against my current.~~

~~You do not~~ (fear) ~~the pull of~~
~~my murky undertow.~~

~~You vow forever to me~~
~~as if it were as simple as~~
~~slipping a ring upon my finger~~
~~because, maybe this time, it is.~~

Currently Listening To:
Big Sean, "IDFWU"

154

Track Twenty Seven

~~Some~~ times it hurts ~~to breathe.~~

~~My corrupt decisions~~
~~weigh on my chest,~~
~~methodically pushing down~~
~~to crack each rib,~~
~~in hopes of infiltrating~~
~~my heart and finally exterminating~~
~~the last shred of~~ the human being
~~I once was.~~

~~If that happens,~~
~~if my sanctuary is breached,~~
~~I will not stand a chance.~~

~~I will lose the one last single atom~~
~~that makes me, me.~~

~~I can't lose me.~~
~~I'm all I've got.~~

Currently Listening To:
The Killers, "All These Things That I've Done"

Track Twenty Eight

~~Growing up, my mother cautioned I would not possess the power to plan out my life.~~

(I) ~~couldn't say,~~
~~I'll be married by X,~~
~~have a kid by Y,~~
~~have a book out by Z.~~

(I was told) ~~as much as I crave to treat my life as one big to-do list,~~ (I would) ~~instead find myself asking,~~
~~Where from here? at least a few times in my life.~~

~~Now, I catch myself asking this a few times a day.~~

~~Where from here?~~

~~Three pint-sized words shouldn't be able to pose such a fatal and final question, but alas, they do. If you go right, you can't go left. Even if you backpedal to take the other route just a second later, your fate will already be altered. It's this or that, never both. It is a hard pill for me to swallow, but I do believe it is in the navigation that you find your way, and~~ (inevitably)
(find you) ~~self.~~

Currently Listening To:
Dean Martin, "You Belong to Me"

Track Twenty Nine

I carry you with me all of the time,
but I feel your absence most on the
days when I'm the happiest.

Not when I need you here the most,
but when I want you here the most.

I believe grief is like a shadow.

It's always there, it follows
you everywhere you go,
but you only see it when
the sun is shining on a beautiful day.

Currently Listening To:
Aaliyah, "I Don't Wanna"

Track Thirty

A change in the season
always ignited a change
in your heart.

I became angry with the Universe
and its natural transitions.

I came to fear
our altered rhythm,
the subtle shifts
in both your affection
and in the air.

Seasons
have
patterns.

You'd be back.

And like winter's
losing fight
against spring,

I'd thaw.

Currently Listening To:
Doris Day, "Que Sera, Sera (Whatever Will Be, Will Be)"

Track Thirty One

EWR to BNA

The ride to the airport is always too short.

Even if I'm packed for days, I'm never ready to go.
A nervous feeling inhabits my stomach right before
my feet hit the hectic curb.

I check my bag and then head up to security. The
line is long as the employee asks, *Are you alone?*

(In life or just right now?)

He points me in the direction away from
the lovers and families traveling together.

The person in front of me doesn't have to
remove their shoes but I do *(of course)*
so now I'm barefoot in Newark Airport.

I make it to the gate
and immediately insert my headphones.

That doesn't stop the Chatty Cathy beside me
from asking, *So, where are you coming from?*

(Don't you mean, "What are you running from?")

Pretending she startled me, I remove my
headphones. She repeats the question.

~~(How specific do you want me to get? I'm coming from therapy. I'm coming from a weekend of binge-drinking. I'm coming from a sleepless night due to a migraine I'm still feeling.)~~

~~I answer, New Jersey.~~

~~I've always preferred the more hopeful, Where are~~ (you) ~~heading?~~

~~My answer?~~

~~Everywhere.~~

Currently Listening To:
Gavin DeGraw, "Not Over You"

Track Thirty Two

~~There have been nights~~
~~I've shared a twin bed~~ with him
~~and still couldn't get close enough.~~

~~Then there have been nights~~
~~spent in a king bed where I've felt~~
~~as though his annoying ass was still~~
~~in my personal space.~~

~~We ebb and flow.~~
~~But~~ there's no one else ~~I'd rather~~
~~crash into every night when~~
~~the tide hits its inevitable peak.~~

Currently Listening To:
Fort Minor, "Where'd You Go?"

Track Thirty Three

~~I feel at peace~~ the nights
~~I find myself naked~~
~~beneath our sheets.~~

~~I stare at the ceiling,~~
~~and I create my own constellations~~
~~from its paint cracks.~~

I feel ~~more connected to the Universe~~
~~during the moments we spend together~~
~~under our~~ artificial ~~plaster sky~~

~~than I ever could on evenings spent~~
~~outside, with the starry night sky~~

~~counting actual~~
~~constellations~~

without you.

Currently Listening To:
Nirvana, "Where Did You Sleep Last Night?"

Track Thirty Four

~~Not laughing for fear of crying.~~
~~Not loving for fear of heartbreak.~~
~~Not choosing for fear of wrong decisions.~~
~~Not dreaming for fear of nightmares.~~
~~Not trusting for fear of betrayal.~~
~~Not jumping for fear of broken bones.~~
~~Not exploring for fear of~~ (getting lost)

~~Not attempting for fear of failing~~
~~is like not living for fear of dying.~~

~~It~~ is impossible to escape ~~this world unscathed.~~

~~So, embrace this m e s s y,~~
~~un   certain   existence~~

~~and live.~~

Currently Listening To:
Missy Higgins, "Where I Stood"

Track Thirty Five

~~I'm not the one who got away.~~

~~Late nights and loneliness~~
~~have built me up in your head.~~

~~Let~~ting go of ~~even~~ the wrong heart
~~can play tricks on one's mind,~~
~~confusing~~ two ~~souls that~~
~~once mated for soul mates.~~

~~So, please, the next time~~
~~the smell of Chanel fills up a room~~
~~and you~~ find you~~rself~~
~~reminded of me, remember:~~

~~I never even wore perfume.~~

Currently Listening To:
Mumford & Sons, "Awake My Soul"

Track Thirty Six

~~I find comfort~~
~~in the colors of a sunset.~~

I find a special magic
in ~~the fact~~
~~it never photographs~~
~~as beautifully as my eyes~~
~~can witness it firsthand.~~

~~I find a certain peace~~
~~in the conclusion of~~
~~another day lived.~~

~~And I find hope~~
~~in the precarious promise~~
~~of~~ tomorrow.

Currently Listening To:
Billy Joel, "The Longest Time"

Track Thirty Seven

~~Four children sit together in a room,~~
~~forming a square.~~

~~In the center is a deck of cards. Brand new.~~
~~Together, using all fifty-two, they construct a~~
~~house of cards.~~

~~They revel at their masterpiece for all of two~~
~~minutes, as one of their mothers enters the room.~~
~~Believing it to be muggy, she opens the window.~~

~~A gust of wind enters and blows~~
~~the cards in different directions.~~

~~Annoyed a tornado destroyed their work in mere~~
~~seconds, one child storms out of the room, leaving~~
~~the door open. The three remaining children~~
~~decide to start over.~~

~~Card by card the house is reassembled.~~
~~Immediately following, the family's puppy~~
~~charges into the room through the opened door~~
~~and plows into the house of cards like a~~
~~wrecking ball through cement.~~

~~Another one of the children runs out in tears.~~

~~The remaining two children once again collect the~~
~~fifty-two cards and begin to form the foundation.~~

And just as the final card is placed on top,
the mother reappears and swings the
playroom door closed.

Though brief, the sudden, manufactured airstream
causes the house to collapse for the third time just
as the door slams shut.

This setback causes another child
to march out of the room.

A single child begins gathering the cards.

Her mother comes in and asks why she is playing
alone when all her friends are outside.

Without even a hesitation, the child responds,
*If I still have the pieces, why wouldn't I keep
rebuilding?*

Currently Listening To:
Sara Evans, "A Little Bit Stronger"

Track Thirty Eight

No matter how old I become, a slight sadness always washes over me moments before I drive away from the home where I grew up.

Feelings of melancholy enter the pit of my stomach as though I am saying goodbye to a dear friend. I stand at the curb soaking in the last moments of hearing my mother's wind chimes sway in the autumnal air.

It is likely I will live in a few different houses throughout my life, but I believe there will always only be one *home* for me.

A home where memories have seeped deep into the paint and pillows; where unconditional love travels around the house as if it were another member of the family.

A sanctuary where pictures, unchanged for years, hang on the wall as reminders of who I used to be and how far I have come.

There is something different about the breeze that passes through the windows of my parents' home it somehow holds the power to wrap around me and rock me until I drift off to sleep.

~~That cozy security felt by sharing a bedroom wall with my sister. There's something reassuring about seeing my mother's purse slung over a kitchen chair or my father's shoes by the front door.~~

~~In a world where so many unfamiliar variables can arise out of nowhere, it is a comfort to have a very familiar constant.~~

~~*Home*, where love and support concurrently grounded me and encouraged me to fly.~~

Currently Listening To:
Haley Reinhart, "Can't Help Falling in Love with You"

Track Thirty Nine

I was running ~~errands the day I received the worst news of my life. I got the phone call in Target's parking lot, hung up, got out of my car, puked on the side of my tire, and still walked into the store to buy the birthday card I needed.~~

~~Now, in the past, I have cried hysterically~~ from happiness. ~~I have laughed uncontrollably out of immense anger. And I have been so overly tired that I was u~~n~~able to sleep.~~

~~But as the red-vested cashier asked the usual,~~
H~~ow~~ *~~are you today?~~*

~~I responded,~~
~~Fine, thanks.~~

~~And somehow~~
I ~~even managed to~~ smile.

Currently Listening To:
Snow Patrol, "Run"

Track Forty

There are days I spill coffee
all over the passenger seat before 7 a.m.

Days I forget to pay bills
or respond to wedding invitations.

Days I am overwhelmingly sad
for reasons I cannot pinpoint.

Day I will no doubt attempt to pull
a door clearly marked *Push.*

Most days I find myself stumbling
over flat surfaces and expectations.

Yet, I know you will love me the same,
and that alone makes my daily
missteps less catastrophic.

Eternally Grateful,
Your Hot Mess

Currently Listening To:
Coldplay, "The Scientist"

171

Track Forty One

~~A message from~~ the Universe ~~appeared in the form of a handwritten note taped to the wall of a nail salon.~~

~~We are not responsible for your loss.~~

I knew the ~~makeshift sign simply forewarned if I left behind one of my possessions it was my fault, not theirs. Yet, I took it to mean more, as if the world was shaking me awake.~~

~~I need to stop making~~ excuses.

~~I need to stop placing blame.~~ I ~~need to stop renaming the decisions I've~~ made ~~as mistakes just because I wish I could take them back.~~

Currently Listening To:
Ryn Weaver, "Promises"

Track Forty Two

I never wanted to help you
with your problems
because I am selfish.

I knew if I were to let you go,
that alone would solve
every single issue in your life,
and I just wasn't ready
to leave you yet.

Currently Listening To:
Sugarland, "Stay"

Track Forty Three

See *you* ~~later,~~ Cuz.

The last words my cousin ~~ever~~ said to me.

~~Last words.~~
~~What~~ an unusual concept.

~~We rarely know they are the last~~
~~as they leave lips.~~

~~Though it was a dark time,~~
~~I am certain she believed~~
~~in her last words~~ to me.

~~I am certain she believed~~
~~there would be another day.~~

~~Her last words were a promise.~~

~~And though, yes,~~ we ~~will never~~
~~see each other again in the physical,~~
~~I do believe I see my cousin all around me.~~

~~In dusty Emerson books~~
~~and in old Broadway ticket stubs.~~

~~In magazines we used to thumb through.~~

In her mother's laugh.
In an eye-roll after hearing
her father's latest joke.
In a drive by a lake.
In yellowed photographs.
In the steep hill of her front lawn.

In shopping for CDs
and cheesy Sandra Bullock movies.

In ponytails and black hoodies.
In the title song from *Rent*.

In sushi dinners in New York City.

In Christmas mornings
and sarcastic remarks.

In an order of buffalo fries (*extra spicy*).

In Goo Goo Dolls song lyrics.

And most importantly, in my heart.

I use my words as a vessel to reach her.
To stay connected to her.
To keep her connected to us.
To hold up my end of our promise.

I will see you later, Cuz.

Currently Listening To:
Selena Gomez, "The Heart Wants What It Wants"

Track Forty Four

~~The sand beneath my feet~~
(belongs) ~~to September now.~~
~~The salt air I inhale~~
~~belongs~~ (to) ~~September now.~~
~~The crashing waves~~
~~belong to September now.~~

~~August can have~~
~~my yesterdays;~~
~~my tomorrows~~
~~belong to September now.~~

~~And~~ (my heart)
~~belongs to September now.~~

Currently Listening To:
The Beach Boys, "Wouldn't It Be Nice"

Track Forty Five

~~Dedicated to Kellie.~~

~~Sisters can have very little in common. No shared~~ ~~interests or friends or aspirations. The most~~ (my) ~~sister and I have in common most days are our~~ ~~blue eyes, parents, and my clothes.~~

~~Yet, we are tethered together, unfailingly.~~

~~It's one thing to have a~~ (support system) ~~in your life~~ ~~to cheer you on during the instances when~~ ~~everyone~~ (is rooting for) ~~you. However, it's another~~ ~~thing entirely to look back in your darkest~~ ~~moments and still see them standing in your~~ ~~corner, encouraging you to stay in the ring and~~ ~~FIGHT, when the odds aren't in your favor and all~~ ~~you want to do is throw in the towel.~~

~~Not many people in this life will be on your side~~ ~~even when they aren't on your side. Even less who~~ ~~mo~~(me)~~ntarily will slam doors out of frustration but~~ ~~never actually lock you out.~~

~~Unconditional love, the definition of *sister*.~~

Currently Listening To:
Kanye West, Jay Z, Big Sean, "Clique"

Track Forty Six

Packing up your belongings means nothing
if you can't box up your heart, scribble *fragile*
along the side, and take it with you, too.

It's hard to walk away, even if you know
in your heart of hearts it's necessary.
Even if your feet can't do the job
and you find yourself crawling on
your hands and knees away
from a toxic situation,

be proud of yourself.

You are removing yourself
to better yourself
and you will stand
on your own two feet
again eventually.

So crawl, walk, or run,
the *how* doesn't matter.
Your new life is waiting for you.

Currently Listening To:
Notorius B.I.G., "Juicy"

Track Forty Seven

~~This drugstore lipstick~~
~~is doing a poor job at covering~~
~~my chapped, bitten lips.~~

~~My sunglasses~~
~~are doing their best to hide~~
~~the dark circles surrounding my light eyes.~~

~~*Would the wind feel this cold today*~~
~~*if you were still here?*~~

(I) ~~think back to the last real day we spent together,~~
~~there was nothing special about it. It was rushed,~~
~~and I~~ (remember the) ~~coffee tasting bitter. It's only~~
~~special now because it was our last.~~

~~Though I wish we had traded~~
~~everlasting~~ (last words, we didn't.)
~~And we won't.~~

~~However, now when I have a cup~~
~~of bad coffee, it will taste less bitter~~
~~and more sweet. I will smile and savor it,~~
~~like the last real day we~~ (shared) ~~together.~~

Currently Listening To:
Plain White T's, "Radios in Heaven"

Track Forty Eight

~~I was the kind of kid~~
~~who would step on ants~~
~~and then ask my mother~~
~~if their family~~
~~would miss them.~~

~~When~~ I ~~was ten,~~
~~I begged my parents~~
~~for a typewriter~~
~~and then had my father~~
~~show me how to~~
~~draft a professional résumé.~~

~~When I was eleven,~~
~~I coerced my siblings~~
~~and cousins~~
~~to perform skits~~
~~and lip-synch in music videos~~
~~I filmed with~~
~~the family camcorder.~~

~~When I was thirteen,~~
~~I would spend hours~~
~~after school writing~~
~~original stories~~
~~using the characters~~
~~from *Buffy the Vampire Slayer*~~

~~and the members of~~
~~the Backstreet Boys.~~
~~I had no idea~~
~~it was called~~
~~*fan fiction* at the time.~~

~~I was a witch~~
~~for Halloween six times,~~
~~not because~~
~~I lacked creativity,~~
~~but because~~
~~I~~ desperately wanted
~~to be a witch.~~
~~Like, *for real.*~~

~~One day,~~
~~my uncle looked at me~~
~~and said,~~
~~*You're a lonely soul, man.*~~
~~It's possible,~~
~~I suppose.~~

~~I studied English~~
~~in a Catholic women's college~~
~~and, for my senior thesis,~~
~~rewrote *Alice in Wonderland*~~
~~from the White Rabbit's perspective.~~

~~I also explored in writing~~
the idea of ~~Anna Karenina~~

~~being pushed under the carriage~~
~~of that passing train~~
~~against her will.~~

~~My professor told me~~
~~I didn't listen to~~
~~the essay instructions.~~

~~I got the paper back~~
~~and saw that I earned an A anyway~~
~~with a note saying,~~

~~Alicia, though~~ you ~~blatantly~~
~~ignored the prompt, after reading~~
~~this succinct conspiracy theory,~~
~~I can see the original essay topic~~
~~would have bored you.~~
~~Does your brain~~
~~ever slow down?~~

~~No.~~

Currently Listening To:
Bobby Brown, "My Prerogative"

Track Forty Nine

I love the way your tongue curls when
you are about to sneeze. I love that you don't
sit on the same side of the booth as me when
we are out to dinner. I love how you pretend
to notice my manicure.

And I love that I cannot
define the word *love*
without saying your name.

Anytime I am anywhere,
I wish you were beside me
because I am unable to separate
my life from yours.

Which leads me to believe you are my life,
and my life is you;

they are one and the same.

Currently Listening To:
A Fine Frenzy, "Almost Lover"

Track Fifty

~~The shore is~~ always ~~forgiving of the sea,~~
~~though they merge together,~~
~~time~~ and ~~time again only to part.~~

~~The sea always~~ returns ~~to kiss the shore,~~
~~for both hold the innate understanding~~
~~that one cannot exist without the other.~~

~~We forgive~~ each other ~~for the very same reason.~~

Currently Listening To:
Luther Vandross, "I'd Rather"

Track Fifty One

~~I wear my~~ (yesterday).

~~Yesterday's hair.~~
~~Yesterday's clothes.~~
~~Yesterday's makeup.~~

~~You.~~

~~My yesterdays are familiar but each day~~ (the)
~~become more wrinkled, worn, and stained~~
~~and bring me less comfort. My~~ (past) ~~is~~
~~beginning to feel tight around my neck — itchy.~~

~~I like to believe I am outgrowing who I was~~
~~and what I needed when I was that person.~~

~~I like to think I will~~ (shed) ~~all of this,~~
~~even the skin you've touched.~~

(It)~~'s nice to think about.~~

Currently Listening To:
Ella Henderson, "All Again"

185

Track Fifty Two

It's commonplace
to ramble off *I lost myself,*
when you go off course.

It's the perfect excuse,
one that allows you to admit fault
while simultaneously remaining the victim.

I admit I've even said it
after I fucked up
beyond a simple apology
and had to look my
collateral damage in the eyes.

Is that bullshit though?
Did I lose myself or just lose focus?
Did I become selfish,
even but for a moment,
and destroy something?

Perhaps we give so much of ourselves
away that we feel like essential pieces
of ourselves go missing.

We give ourselves away
to our past regrets and present aspirations,
to missed opportunities and everyday miracles,

to lovers and ex-lovers,
to harsh realities and unattainable daydreams,
to lost childhoods and ill-prepared adulthoods,
to flat tires and missed trains,
to friends and enemies,
to happy birthdays and hungover mornings,
to families and their fallen faces
when we let them down,
to fall festivities,
winter wonderlands,
sprung springs,
and summer suns.

I do not believe we lose ourselves.

I'd like to think we would never lose
something so precious if we could help it.

That, my friends,
I think life steals from us
from time to time.

Currently Listening To:
Maren Morris, "I Could Use a Love Song"

Track Fifty Three

(My) ~~brain is~~

~~all~~
~~over~~
~~the   place.~~

~~Grief will do that to you.~~

~~Today I sat in my car in my own driveway~~
~~for twenty minutes staring blankly~~
~~at my glove compartment.~~

~~My mind d r i f t e d o f f.~~

~~Grief will do that to you.~~

~~I found myself wondering why we still call this~~
~~thing a "glove compartment" when no one keeps~~
~~driving gloves, or any gloves for that matter, in~~
~~there anymore.~~

~~As a society, we are always talking about~~
(progression.) ~~We are renaming TV stations and~~
~~street names—but can't rename this storage box~~
~~within our cars.~~

~~Don't fix what~~ (ain't broken) ~~I guess.~~

~~Something broke me, and I need to be fixed.~~

~~Grief will do that to you.~~

~~What else would we call it?~~

~~Crumpled tissue holder.~~
~~Registration and insurance safe.~~

~~I question everything now,~~
~~even things that don't matter.~~

~~Grief will do that to you.~~

Currently Listening To:
Eminem, "Legacy"

Track Fifty Four

One daybreak I woke to the aftermath of a surprise snowstorm. It was one of those storms that visit overnight when you least expect it, like in the middle of March even though the weather has warmed and you've stopped wearing a coat.

There was a lot of snow,
but the plows had arrived already.

I guess it wasn't as unexpected as I thought.

I got in my car and began my commute to work. It takes me through a park. That morning the park was blanketed in virgin snow. The bare trees wore the flakes like diamond earrings.

Everything was clean and beautiful,
white and pure.

It reminded me of snow days spent home from school. It reminded me of the fifteen minutes it took to suit up before going outside. It reminded me of snow angels and snow-adorned railroad tracks. It reminded me of the chill felt when ice would sneak inside my glove and shock my wrist. It reminded me of my mother laying our wet clothes on the radiators to dry.

I urged myself to pull over and take a picture of the beauty. That's how much the vision moved me. I wanted to stop and capture the scene, but I didn't. I was already driving too slow to make it to work on time so I just kept driving. The adult in me had won over my inner child. I promised myself I would take a picture on my ride back home — back through the same park.

As I sat at my desk that day, the temperature crept up and I watched the snow melt. I felt sad. By the time I was driving back through the park, everything was brown and dry again — litter was exposed — all the beauty had melted away. I should have stopped all of three seconds to take that damn picture. Who knows if I will see a winter wonderland like that again in my lifetime.

Thirty years old and I still think a moment will wait for me to catch up.

Currently Listening To:
Whitney Houston, "All at Once"

Track Fifty Five

I spent a lot of my early twenties
making mistakes,
really bad ones.

The light of day was not my friend;
I was tired of how it illuminated my missteps.

I began plucking away at my blessings
like stars from the sky
just so my world could go black.

Enlightenment was something
I bumped into in the dark,
like a corner of a table or lamp.

Isolating yourself
does not make you unique,
it makes you a coward,
too afraid or ashamed
to show up for your own life.

I decided a long time ago
to stop exclusively chasing
my visions just when
my head was on a pillow.

I decided a long time ago
to be better off in the daylight.

~~To do better,~~
~~to be better,~~
~~to make other~~
~~things better.~~

~~My whole damn life~~
~~is~~ (my) ~~passion project.~~

~~You think I have big hair,~~
~~you should see my~~ (dreams)

Currently Listening To:
Big Sean, "Bounce Back"

Track Fifty Six

~~What is the difference between Earth~~
~~and the World? I asked my fourth grade~~
~~teacher whose name escapes me.~~

~~She seemed to be using~~
~~the terms interchangeably.~~

~~Since,~~ *right now,*
~~humans only live~~
~~here on Earth,~~
~~the two words mean~~
~~the same thing,~~
~~she answered.~~

~~As years went on,~~ I ~~found the two words to be~~
~~vastly different. Earth is the planet we inhabit,~~
~~yes, but the World is a unique plane of existence~~
~~to each person. As we plant roots and find love~~
~~and birth babies and become regulars at coffee~~
~~shops and restaurants,~~ *the World* ~~quickly~~
~~becomes~~ *Our World;* ~~mini-colonies.~~

~~I've found that certain worlds can become as~~
~~narrow as hallways, and these passages I walk~~
~~through, the worlds I know,~~ can
~~begin to feel constrictive.~~

~~The truth is, I've outgrown many worlds on Planet Earth, only to~~ begin again ~~Earth provides the air we need to fill our lungs, but *Our Worlds* give us every reason to breathe deep. We must not take anything for granted on the exhale.~~

Currently Listening To:
Brandi Carlile, "The Story"

Track Fifty Seven

~~This mirror holds all~~ (my secrets)
~~my hopes and fears are mixed~~
~~with the toothpaste spatter~~
~~I keep~~ (forget)~~ting~~ (to) ~~wipe away.~~

~~It sees me at my most vulnerable,~~
~~crusty eyed and naked face.~~

~~I am forced to face it each day.~~

~~You do not have it all together,~~
~~I write in the steam,~~
~~knowing it will~~ (disappear.)

~~I realize that this may be~~
~~the most honest I will be all day.~~

Currently Listening To:
Mike Posner, "Only God Knows"

Track Fifty Eight

~~You~~ teeth will begin to chatter.
~~Your fingertips will turn blue.~~
~~Your lips will chap~~ and your eyes will tear.

~~You will wonder why~~
~~you just can't shake~~
~~that penetrating chill~~
within ~~your bones.~~

~~It is because~~
my ~~warmth~~
~~left your~~ heart.

Currently Listening To:
Gloria Estefan, "Here We Are"

Track Fifty Nine

I want a busy kitchen, with small fingerprint smudges on the refrigerator door. I want a crowded bed where all nightmares disappear. I want to jump in a cold pool or ocean and still smile. I want early Christmas mornings, with stockings held by the chimney with care and little voices whispering Santa came! I want to be a thirty-something year old in a pointy cardboard birthday hat. I want my homemade chicken noodle soup to cure colds and my Band-Aid kisses to heal knee scrapes. I want to freeze moments in cement. I want to learn to swim again, skip through sprinklers again, welcome the tooth fairy again, and make sand castles again. I want to believe in magic again.

I want to be born again.

Currently Listening To:
The Rolling Stones, "Wild Horses"

Track Sixty

The ~~letters behind the cursor are already in the~~
past ~~That's how fast it all happens. A finite twenty-six~~
~~letters create an infinite trail of breadcrumbs~~
~~that~~ lead ~~to different moments~~ ~~that lead~~ to ~~who~~
~~I was just a moment before.~~

~~I am no longer the~~ person
I ~~was just a twinkling ago.~~

~~The changes are so minute,~~
~~but they are there~~
~~you may think you remain~~
~~the~~ same ~~person you were~~

~~a day ago,~~
~~an hour ago,~~
~~a page ago,~~
~~a line break ago,~~

~~but you are~~ not.

Currently Listening To:
Jewel, "Foolish Games"

Track Sixty One

Maybe you've gone through something
no one should have to go through
at such a young age.

Maybe you know the pain
of a loss so deep,
your marrow aches.

Not many know the anguish felt in

growing older than your older sister.
Having her laugh stolen from you
in the middle of a joke.
Talking in past tense.

Everything will be in
past tense from now on.

Maybe you know what it is like
to wake up from slumber,
covered in your own tears.

Maybe each pump of your heart hurts
your chest, but you heart pumps, even still.

This pain is reminding you
that you are alive.

~~There is an empowerment~~
~~uncorked in grief.~~

~~Your life will never be the same, ever,~~
~~so you can never be the same, ever.~~

~~Pain will make you stronger,~~
~~but it will make you a lot~~
~~of other things first.~~

~~Maybe at its worst,~~
~~it will~~ (cripple) ~~you;~~

~~but, maybe,~~
~~at its best,~~
~~it will bec~~(me)
~~your superpower.~~

Currently Listening To:
Kid Rock, "Picture"

201

Track Sixty Two

Growth ~~or a change~~
~~in my perspective~~
~~will turn some people off,~~
~~turn some people away.~~

~~This~~ doesn't ~~mean~~
~~I am growing in the wrong direction.~~
~~It's important to remember~~
~~no one needs to be in my corner~~
~~as long as I am in my corner.~~
~~No one needs to witness my~~ come ~~back,~~
~~what matters is I come back.~~

~~This~~ is ~~not a classic underdog story,~~
~~I am not a phoenix.~~
~~I did not rise from the ashes~~
~~I crawled out from under the soot,~~

~~fingernails cracked,~~
~~palms bloody,~~
~~face muddy.~~

~~I told you I'd be okay~~ one day.
~~Today is that day.~~

Currently Listening To:
Imagine Dragons, "I Bet My Life"

Track Sixty Three

If you ever left,
~~in rhyme.~~

~~The wind would still come~~
~~and the chimes would still play.~~
~~The sun would still rise~~
and the moon would end the day.
~~The waves would still crash~~
~~and the gulls would still caw.~~

~~But I,~~
~~I wouldn't be the same.~~
~~Not at all.~~

Currently Listening To:
Incubus, "I Miss You"

Track Sixty Four

~~I have begun measuring~~ life
~~not just in numbers~~
~~and years~~
~~but~~ in ~~sunsets and~~
~~trees blossoming~~ a ~~nd~~
~~brilliant views.~~

~~You cannot calculate my growth by the notches~~
~~etched in the molding of my bedroom wall. You~~
~~cannot understand my scars by the nicks on my~~
~~knees and elbows. You cannot grasp my~~
metamorphosis ~~by the skin I've shed or~~
~~the baby teeth I've lost.~~

~~It can~~ not ~~be determined in~~ a ~~nything I've lost or~~
~~in what's marred me. It can only be quantified in~~
~~what remains, in what withstood every storm~~
~~and every~~ disruption ~~of my heart.~~

~~You can see my growth simply by the fact that I~~
~~am still standing here, believing that this world~~
~~is still an inherently good place to laugh, to hurt,~~
~~to love, to lose, to exist.~~

Currently Listening To:
Oasis, "Wonderwall"

Track Sixty Five

~~EWR to UAU~~

~~You know something bad happened last night,~~
~~but you don't pry. You figure I'll bring it up~~
~~when I'm ready. We board the flight. We take~~
~~off. I~~ (remember) ~~mumbling something to you~~
~~about how I never sleep on planes (granted, I~~
~~haven't slept in my own bed in some time,~~
~~either). Suddenly, my body shuts down and I~~
~~slump onto your shoulder. Sleep found me~~
~~before 30,000 feet. I wake a bit startled, a bit~~
~~surprised, and for~~ (the first time) ~~in weeks (or has~~
~~it been years?), a bit rested. My mind was finally~~
~~able to rest, knowing I was flying far away from~~
~~here. You offer me your neck pillow~~ (and a smile.)

Currently Listening To:
Jimmy Eat World, "Work"

Track Sixty Six

I am under construction. Not many people like to admit that, but everyone is always in the process of becoming something else. No one is ever really finished — constructed and complete.

I am starting to sleep at a normal hour again. So that probably means I am healing. Sleep is the first thing to leave you after something like this. Sanity follows soon after. The loss of one is definitely directly related to the loss of the other.

I still have some trouble getting out of bed come morning, but I learned what matters most is getting out of bed at all. I've read about people who were so sad, they stayed in bed all day. That alone motivated me to want to get up, even if I just moved to the couch. The couch is not the bed.

A lot of what I knew left with you, and that made me tired. Ask any school-aged child, learning new things at times can be frustrating and draining. It hasn't been a fluid progression of bad to better, but my repaired days have begun to outnumber my damaged ones.

Currently Listening To:
Drake, "Weston Road Flows"

Track Sixty Seven

I used to love hotel rooms.
Now, the sheets feel stiff
and the unacquainted features
of the room do not hold the same allure.

The white bedding
doesn't smell like the wet towel
you absentmindedly left on our bed.

The pillowcases
don't hold the distinct scent
of your raven hair.

The air doesn't smell
like your cologne.

The closet
holds a dripping iron
but your sneakers are nowhere to be found.

The room service I ordered
doesn't include you,
sipping coffee across from me,
asking me about my day.

Currently Listening To:
Little Big Town, "Girl Crush"

207

Track Sixty Eight

To the guy who fell asleep on the couch.

We're private, many can't understand why we don't share every second of our lives with the masses. Many get excited to have a wedding, and wear the pretty dress, and put on the expensive rings, but that one day in the scheme of "forever" that is celebrated annually doesn't really matter. The stuff to really celebrate comes after that day. Choosing to stay together. To work on things. I've got to be one of the most difficult people to love and remain in love with, I'm sometimes selfish and my chaotic thoughts translate into the mess I leave around our house. I'm independent in most aspects of my life but totally dependent when it comes to you. Without you, I'd fall apart. Some time ago, I decided on forever, and I am so very fortunate you did, too.

Currently Listening To:
The Turtles, "Happy Together"

Track Sixty Nine

~~Memories~~ ~~are mere echoes~~
~~of the actual occurrence.~~
~~Distorted in the reverberation.~~
~~Romanticized in the ricochet.~~

~~My ghost towns were~~ ~~crowded~~
~~for such a long time.~~
~~You don't haunt me anymore.~~
~~Memory lane is just another street~~
~~I turn left at on~~ ~~my way~~ ~~to~~
~~the grocery store now.~~

~~I prefer it this way.~~

Currently Listening To:
Céline Dion, "It's All Coming Back to Me Now"

Track Seventy

~~Scraped knees. Black eyes.~~ *Tears.*

~~This is all pain we can see. Pain we can aid.~~
~~Pain that will heal if we tend and mend.~~

~~Then, there is *that other pain*.~~

~~The pain so embedded into our being, so deep,~~
~~that it fuses to our existence~~ and ~~mixes with our~~
~~bloodstream. It doesn't just become a part of us,~~
~~it becomes who we are.~~

~~It's that other~~ pain ~~you can't see that never~~
~~really heals, not fully anyway. It's also the pain~~
~~that gives us a higher purpose. The kind of pain~~
~~that~~ will turn you into a warrior.

~~Those mascara streaks are your war paint;~~
~~wear them proudly.~~

Currently Listening To:
Sia, "Bird Set Free"

Track Seventy One

I am too focused on my next move to worry about what everyone on earth is doing next. I don't need to beat down who I was yesterday, or anyone else for that matter, to grow. I don't take advantage of the disadvantages of others. I refuse to race against time, other women, or men. I can only reach my next level, not anyone else's.

I compete with my own benchmarks,
my own comfort zones,
my own inner strength,
and my own voice.

Currently Listening To:
John Lennon, "Imagine"

Track Seventy Two

I have demanded to speak to God directly three
times. Three times in three decades is not a lot,
I'd say. I found Him the other night, in a
different place than I found Him last.

The first time I found Him wading within
the crests of waves of water too cold to swim.
The second time, I found Him sleeping
inside the thread count of my beloved's sheets.

This time I found Him stitched into
the song of my mother's wind chimes.

I had gone outside to catch my breath.

Outside there is more air,
enough air to save me.

I had my heartbreak,
I had my breakdown,
now I needed my breakthrough.

At that very moment,
the unmistakable wind that bridged seasons
blew through my unwashed hair
and the trees and the metal cylinders
my mother attached to their branches
and He sang to me.

~~His melody calmed me~~
~~and I was able to hear the crickets~~
~~and my family conversing at the dinner table~~
~~and the stati~~ (from) ~~my father's record player~~
~~over the pounding in~~ (my head and heart) ~~again.~~

~~I was brought out of the past~~
~~and placed into the present.~~

~~That's the thing about faith;~~
~~if you are looking,~~
~~you will find it;~~

~~if you need it,~~
~~you will find it;~~

~~if you believe,~~
~~you will find it.~~

Currently Listening To:
Christina Ariana Grande, "Dangerous Woman"

213

Track Seventy Three

~~Yesterday was~~ (a good day.) ~~I woke up easy, slow.~~
~~The smell from the air conditioner in my~~
~~window welcomed me like the warm~~
~~aroma of coffee brewing.~~

~~Yesterday was a good day. The~~ (fore)~~cast called for~~
~~rain, but the sun shined all day. I read a book in~~
~~my hammock. The battery in my phone lasted an~~
~~impressive seven hours. The clothes I ordered~~
~~got delivered and everything fit perfectly.~~

~~Yesterday was a good day. The barista made my~~
~~latte perfectly and there was no line at the~~
~~pharmacy. There were no shadows, no ominous~~
~~clouds, and three of my favorite songs played in~~
~~a row on the radio.~~

~~Yesterday was~~ (a good day)
~~even though you didn't come back.~~

~~My heart noticed the shift~~
~~and smiled.~~

Currently Listening To:
Ice Cube, "It Was a Good Day"

Track Seventy Four

~~I am the most put together broken person you~~
~~will ever come across; with hairline fractures so~~
~~fine~~ (my) ~~skin remains smooth to the touch. I see~~
~~I am shattered,~~ (broken) ~~shards placed together~~
~~and called art, a mosaicked woman.~~

~~Are you having another one of your dark days?~~
~~My father asks.~~

~~Days in a daze become weeks of being weak.~~
~~Months become moths that eat holes into my~~
~~favorite moments.~~

~~There was a time I laughed more, was more~~
~~lighthearted and whimsical. There was a time I~~
~~smiled in more than just pictures. There was~~
(once) ~~a time I at least attempted to end pieces on~~
~~high notes.~~

~~I'll get back there.~~
~~See? A high note.~~

Currently Listening To:
Aaliyah, "The One I Gave My Heart To"

Track Seventy Five

The ocean resides outside where my parents
stay. I breathe in deep. I like the smell of
summer, but the thought of winter
keeps me warm.

December was when you loved me last. Your
mind shifted from me before your heart left. The
crashing waves sound like the dishes I threw
against the wall that night.

If I am broken, the plates we eat
on should be broken, too.

Seagulls caw in the distance,
and I am tired.

Tired of tirelessly crying
over the same old bullshit story.

I love you,
but not right now.

I want you,
but not right now.

The humidity in the air has caused
my footprints to create a trail on the tile.

Now my mother is going to be able to tell
I have been walking in circles.

I've always preferred hardwood floors
but being so close to the ocean doesn't allow it.
The salt in the air can cause
structural damage to the wood,
any beach kid knows this.

I've always preferred you over any other man
but being so close to you doesn't allow it.
The hurt in the air can cause
structural damage to my heart,
any brokenhearted woman knows this.

Currently Listening To:
Mandy Moore, "Cry"

217

Track Seventy Six

~~Darkness is like a sleeping bear—~~
~~it should not be poked, provoked.~~

~~Still, too many~~ (I) ~~know are hunting~~
~~down nightmares, pissing away the~~ (same)
~~time life allots to chase~~ (dreams)

~~I can't take it anymore, honestly,~~
~~all this darkness.~~

~~I have lost my voice—~~
~~trying to convince people I love~~
~~of their own potential.~~

~~I have been the collateral damage~~
~~to a number of life tragedies~~
~~that were not directly my own.~~

~~I've swept up~~ (messes) ~~I haven't created~~
(and) ~~dried~~ (tears) ~~I haven't cried.~~
~~I've aged just by witnessing others lose years.~~

~~Self-destruction destroys~~
~~more than just the individual.~~

Currently Listening To:
Daya, "Sit Still, Look Pretty"

Track Seventy Seven

~~Let's be clear, I did no~~ accidently ~~step into my life. I loved~~ and ~~worked every single day. A good thing happening to a good person is not~~ luck. ~~Just like how a bad thing happening to a bad person is not bad luck. Sometimes,~~ it's just life. ~~I've been hurt. I've cried into my pillow. I've experienced loss. I have been overlooked and underestimated more times than I'd like to admit. I have experienced moments of good fortune.~~

~~Life is all about balance.~~
I ~~am a firm~~ believe~~r that you get what you give~~ in this world.

~~Yes, I am loved~~
~~because I love.~~
~~Yes, I am taken care of~~
~~because I take care of others.~~
~~Yes, I have friends~~
~~because I am a friend.~~

~~I am not going to apologize for my life,~~
~~just like how life did not apologize~~
~~to me when things weren't going my way.~~

Currently Listening To:
Frankie Ballard, "It All Started with a Beer"

Track Seventy Eight

I hollowed out my memory,
to make room for what's to come.

I scooped out the gunk,
the let downs, the heartache,
and left the happiness

Yet, I was no longer myself,
unbalanced.

Maybe I was meant to be sad, I thought.

I plopped back in the painful
and scooped out the happiness;
the weddings, the graduations,
the moments I laughed until I cried.

Once again I found myself unstable.

We need both.
We need the good
and the bad
to be who we are.

For better or worse, we need both.

Currently Listening To:
Mariah Carey, "Love Takes Time"

Track Seventy Nine

~~You~~ face ~~jolted me from sleep.~~

~~The details do not matter,~~
~~because~~ *you no longer* ~~matter.~~

~~I startled the man sleeping next to me,~~
~~the man who matters.~~

~~What is it? he asked, concerned.~~
~~Nothing. It was just a~~ nightmare.

~~I wasn't lying.~~

Currently Listening To:
Eminem, "Cinderella Man"

Track Eighty

~~I believe in what destroyed me.~~
~~I believe it needed to destroy me.~~
~~My pain is not in vain.~~

~~What I went through~~
~~replaced my backbone,~~
~~once as brittle as a wishbone,~~
~~with a sword.~~

Currently Listening To:
The Beatles, "Birthday"

Track Eighty One

When I was leaving your funeral,
church bells sang announcing
another hour in my life,

another hour lived without you.

Birds chirped
and I heard a sprinkler
spraying water on grass
already too green for its own good.

It would have been a great day
if it wasn't already the worst day of my life.

Across from the church was a playground,
children swung on the swings,
in tune to the bells.

A child's eyes met mine,
they were warm, welcoming.

Not only was life still going on,
it was still smiling at me.

Currently Listening To:
Drake, "Now & Forever"

Track Eighty Two

~~I do believe~~ (the sun) ~~will come out after each storm, though no one~~ (knows) ~~how long one of life's storms will last.~~

~~Could be a passing shower, could be a yearlong monsoon.~~

~~You aren't a fictional green witch, you will not melt if you get a little wet.~~

~~I would say learn to dance in the rain but that's too much of a Goddamn cliché these days; at the very least, find~~ the simple joy of ~~jumping in the puddle~~ (life) ~~creates.~~

Currently Listening To:
The Rascals, "A Beautiful Morning"

Track Eighty Three

Some things slow my world down
but nothing has truly
stopped it from spinning.

I don't give up,
even when I feel defeated
and proclaim,
I give up,
I never really do.

What I've been carrying quietly
on my shoulders for years
you wouldn't be able to hoist
onto your back for one day.

The loudest people in the room
aren't always the most heard,
the people crying the loudest
aren't always the most hurt.

Currently Listening To:
Kalie Shorr, "Fight Like a Girl"

Track Eighty Four

~~I still miss you from time to time.~~

~~What's~~ (changed) (how) ~~I've begun~~
~~to handle *the missing*.~~

~~I've learned that pain passes,~~
~~*the missing, it passes*.~~

~~Much like a dizzy spell,~~
~~I just have to wait until my vision~~
(and) ~~mind clear and the aching clears, too.~~

~~That's how I~~ (healed) ~~.~~

~~I woke up every day,~~
~~cried or didn't cry,~~
~~regained my balance,~~
~~and went the hell on with my day,~~

~~which eventually turned into me~~
~~getting the hell on with my life.~~

Currently Listening To:
Miranda Lambert, "Scars"

Track Eighty Five

~~If~~ you are ~~feeling lost,~~
~~helpless,~~
~~down,~~
~~sad,~~
~~angry,~~
~~betrayed,~~
~~you name it,~~

~~you can rise from it,~~
~~you can create from it,~~
~~you can grow from it.~~

~~I am living proof~~
the ~~most turbulent year of one's life~~
~~could also turn out to be~~
~~the~~ greatest ~~more rewarding year, too.~~

Currently Listening To:
Kacey Musgraves, "Cup of Tea"

Track Eighty Six

~~Some weekend mornings in my new home,~~
~~I wake up to the bark of the dog in the~~
~~connecting yard. When I do, for a second,~~ (I)
~~(believe) it's the bark of my family dog.~~

~~The dog that still sleeps an hour away~~ (in) ~~the~~
~~house where I grew up, with the~~ (family) ~~I see far~~
~~less than I wish. The dog we've had since I was~~
~~thirteen years old. The aging dog who spends~~
~~more time with my parents than I do.~~

~~Now, I know it is not him I hear, but for a~~
~~moment I am back in my old bedroom, in the~~
~~busy home where I shared a wall, computer,~~ (and)
~~clothes with my sister and a bathroom with four~~
~~other people. I am back, hearing pots clanging~~
~~and sauce simmering in my mother's kitchen.~~

~~Then, I fully awake, and I am in my new~~ (home)
~~Though I wake alone in a quiet house some~~
~~mornings, I find comfort in the notion of home.~~
~~You don't have to remember to take Home with~~
~~you when you move on; you carry Home in your~~
~~heart, and on some really lucky days, Home~~
~~visits you through the bark of a stranger's pet.~~

Currently Listening To:
Frank Sinatra, "Have Yourself a Merry Little Christmas"

Track Eighty Seven

I accomplished everything in my life
in spite of you, not because of you

You can't take my happiness from me anymore,
because you are no longer the underlying reason.
You can't take something back from someone
you never even held in your own two hands
in the first place.

You do not hold my happiness.
You do not own my happiness.
I manifest my own happiness.

I came this far on a broken heart
functioning at maybe, on a good day,
forty percent efficiency.

I think you should be nervous
about what I will accomplish once I heal.

The mountains I'll move.
The miles I'll cover.
The skin I'll get under.

Currently Listening To:
98 Degrees, "Because of You"

Track Eighty Eight

I don't belong here;
I'm out of sync with what's around me.
My heart doesn't belong here,
it beats out of time,
like a drum in the wrong song.
Oh, how I wish for a breeze to find me,

I'd scatter like confetti
into the air,
ending up in one million
different places at once.

What a magical escape.

Currently Listening To:
Bruce Springsteen, "Jersey Girl"

Track Eighty Nine

~~He looks in my eyes and he knows~~ he's lost me.
~~No~~ forever but ~~for the next few hours.~~

My ~~state is unfocused,~~
~~the~~ sadness ~~simmering~~ ins~~ide of me~~
~~has boiled to the surface.~~

~~I feel every organ that matters:~~
~~my lungs, my heart, my brain.~~

~~They have become heavy,~~
weighing me down ~~in bed.~~

~~He looks in my eyes and knows~~
~~I'll be back soon enough;~~
~~so he rests beside me,~~
~~making sure he's the first thing~~
~~I will see when my heart wakes up again.~~

Currently Listening To:
Lady Gaga, "Million Reasons"

Track Ninety

I find myself singing
to the rhythm of your breathing.

You know the doors
to all four chambers of my heart.

You know which creak
and which open freely.

Most importantly, you know
how to pry open the jammed doors
so many others confused for locked.

You push with all your might,
and I let you in.

Currently Listening To:
Gavin DeGraw, "You Know Where I'm At"

Track Ninety One

~~Doors remain ajar as long as two people~~ (allow.)
~~Once~~ (someone) ~~makes the decision~~ (to leave)
~~the ajar door slams shut right behind them~~
~~with the wind and the letdowns.~~

(You) ~~cannot reenter~~ (once) ~~this happens.~~
~~You cannot reenter that life ever again.~~

~~You're no longer an invited guest,~~
~~you are an intruder.~~

Currently Listening To:
Cher, "Strong Enough"

Track Ninety Two

~~Gathering rays, seashells, and memories.~~
~~I collect my thoughts along the seashore.~~

~~I place one close to my ear.~~
~~I listen intently.~~

~~Breathe in, breathe out,~~
~~you've made it to the other side.~~

Currently Listening To:
Eli Young Band, "Saltwater Gospel"

About the Author

Alicia Cook is an established author and activist. Her work has appeared on the *Huffington Post* and *CNN*, in *USA TODAY* and *Teen Vogue*, and elsewhere. Her bestselling self-published book of poetry, *Stuff I've Been Feeling Lately*, was a finalist in the 2016 Goodreads Choice Awards, and her series of articles, *The Other Side of Addiction*, which focuses on the direct effect drug addiction has, not only on users, but on their families, is read by millions of people across the country. Cook resides in Newark, New Jersey, where she is the Director of Institutional Communications at Bloomfield College.

www.thealiciacook.com

Andrews McMeel Publishing
a division of Andrews McMeel Universal
1130 Walnut Street, Kansas City, Missouri 64106

www.andrewsmcmeel.com

17 18 19 20 21 BVG 10 9 8 7 6 5 4 3 2 1

ISBN: 978-1-4494-8756-0

Library of Congress Control Number: 2016962985

Editor: Patty Rice
Creative Director: Tim Lynch
Production Editor: Erika Kuster
Production Manager: Cliff Koehler

ATTENTION: SCHOOLS AND BUSINESSES

Andrews McMeel books are available at quantity discounts with bulk purchase for educational, business, or sales promotional use. For information, please e-mail the Andrews McMeel Publishing Special Sales Department: specialsales@amuniversal.com.